Sole's MOM

A Transgender Journey
of Love, Loss and Letting Go

Isabelle Camille

Copyright © 2024 by Isabelle Camille

All rights reserved. No part of this book may be reproduced without written permission from the author except for brief quotations included in reviews and other noncommercial uses permitted by law. For permission requests, please contact the author at isacamille@gmail.com.

ISBN: 978-1-962133-86-9

Platypus Publishing

Printed in the United States of America

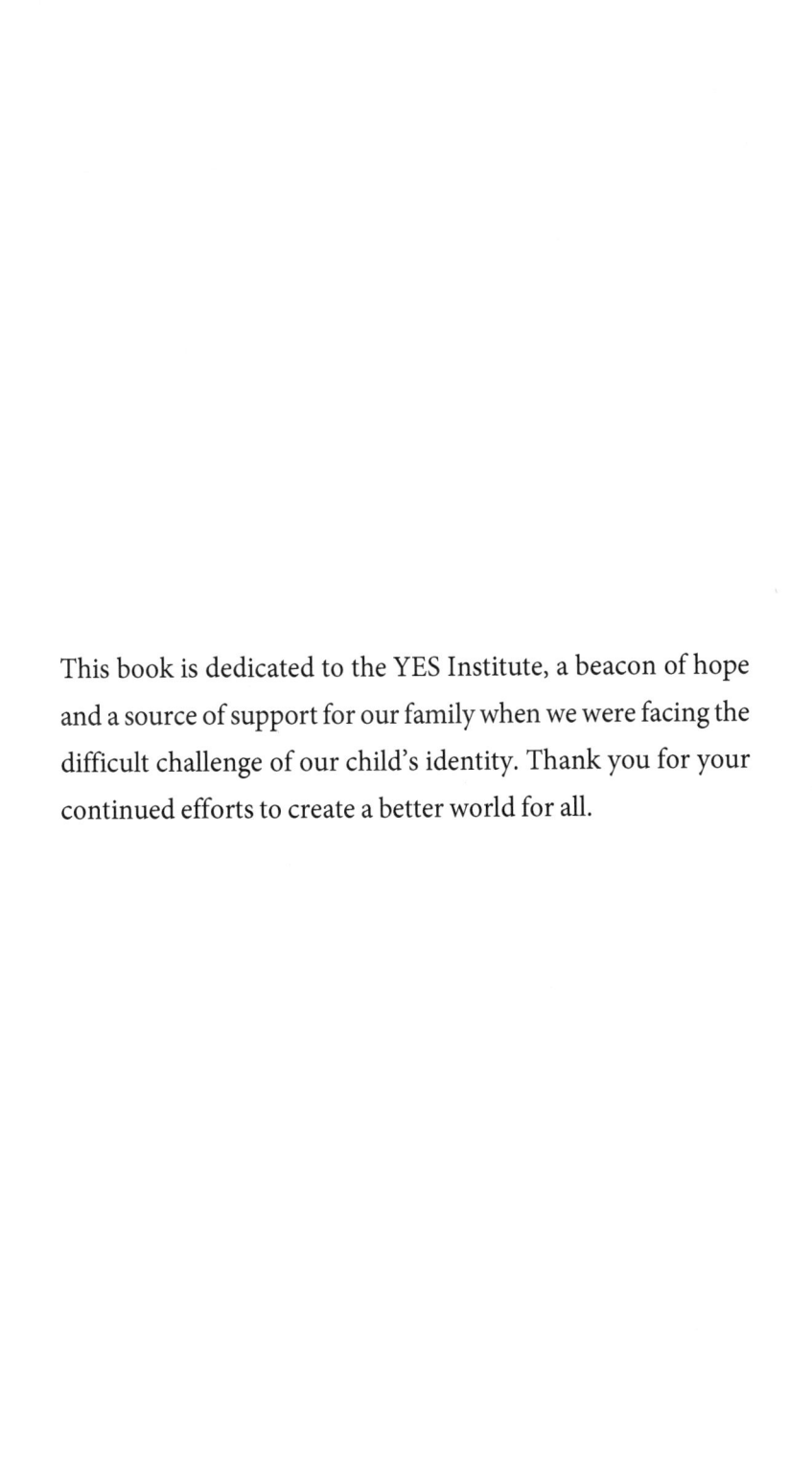

This book is dedicated to the YES Institute, a beacon of hope and a source of support for our family when we were facing the difficult challenge of our child's identity. Thank you for your continued efforts to create a better world for all.

Table of Contents

6	Foreword
10	1. Sole, Not Sky
15	2. The Longing for a Daughter
20	3. Choosing the Name
27	4. The Early Years: A Different Kind of Girl
34	5. Middle School Revelations
49	6. Turbulence in High School
58	7. Beyond Binaries
72	8. Challenging More Norms
84	9. Senior Year
97	10. Giving Ourselves Time
105	11. Confronting and Accepting Change
115	12. Love Ought to Be Enough
123	13. My Sole, My Sky
127	14. Bridging Perspectives
143	About the Author

Foreword

By Lucian Jude

Sky is my brother, and I love him. This book by Sky's mom is a moving testament to the potency of her love for her son, and her willingness to do whatever it takes to keep Sky close to the family and to truly know him—through his gender transition and beyond.

When a child goes through a gender transition, their family, friends, and community go through a transition too. Often, the result is tragic, with relationships irreparably shattered. Sometimes though, relationships become stronger and deeper than ever. Parents, siblings, friends, and neighbors survive the initial shock and tumult and embrace a new reality hand in hand, supporting the transgender child with a fierce protectiveness. When that happens, it seems like magic. But inevitably, there's a champion at the center of the drama who leads the charge toward a happy outcome, who simply refuses to succumb to fear. For my brother Sky, that champion is his mom. And because that's who Isabelle is for Sky, she's my champion too.

Sky and I are unlikely brothers, no doubt. I'm white, 45 years old, and—having grown up on a farm in the Midwest—crave open spaces, solitude, and predictable routines. Sky is Black, 32, and a self-described "nomad" who travels as much as possible when he's not with family and friends in his frenetic hometown of Miami, Florida.

We are, in many ways, from different worlds. But we are brothers, no question. Not by blood, but rather through a shared intimacy that stems from repeatedly breathing life into each other at pivotal moments in our lives. It started the moment Sky and I met.

At that time, I was in the early stages of my gender transition, with a lingering femininity in my physical features that testosterone had yet to erase. Though I was feeling more comfortable in my skin every day, I knew I was still considered "not human" by people who couldn't quickly categorize me as "he" or "she." I felt scared, alone, excited, hopeful, and supremely anxious every waking second.

I was co-leading an educational workshop, and I shared my experience around gender as part of a discussion focused on bullying prevention. When the workshop ended, Sky walked confidently up to me and said some version of, "I'm like you." His face beamed with relief, joy, hope, and anticipation. He radiated aliveness and was devoid of the judgment, curiosity, and revulsion I had come to expect from strangers. With that sustained, intense, and loving gaze, he gave me a place to belong and a purpose big enough to pull me forward. He didn't pepper me with questions or ask anything of me at all. He simply declared himself, and—in doing so—silently communicated, "I see you as who you are, and that's enough." At the time, that was a lifeline for me.

And I knew that I offered a lifeline of sorts to him as well. He saw in me, I think, a hopeful future where he too could have a job, a healthy romantic relationship, and a chance to live true to himself. In that initial meeting, I didn't question Sky, challenge him, or demand evidence, but rather created space for him to experience being seen for the first time without needing to pretend. In that moment, Sky came to life. Witnessing that awakening is something I will always treasure. Our exchange that day was brief, but it cemented a lifetime bond between us.

Since then, Sky has gracefully navigated many challenges, the most impactful being his relationships with his parents. Isabelle describes in this book the big expectations she had for Sky. And Sky felt the weight of those expectations. Like all transgender children, he knew that living true to himself—the only way to go forward now that he had tasted freedom and lightness—might cost him the relationships he held most dear.

Understandably, Sky's gender transition shook Isabelle to the core. But she used her fears and confusion as fuel to learn and reflect—and ultimately surrender to not knowing and loving anyway. Isabelle generously recounts the steps she took to arrive at a place of—perhaps not peace—but resolute clarity about who she wants to be for Sky. And like many parents of transgender children, Isabelle describes her process as coming to terms with losing a daughter (or son, as the case may be). I am not a parent. I don't presume to grasp the pain and fear and questioning that Isabelle went through after learning she had a transgender child. Clearly though, no one died. Sky has always been himself. So in my eyes—for whatever it's worth—Isabelle is embracing the opportunity to know the beautiful son she's always had.

Her vulnerability and courage shine through in these pages. If you have a loved one questioning gender or pursuing a gender transition, you will find value in Isabelle's words. Your path will be unique, of course, but I invite you to pull from Isabelle's strength, wisdom, and patience. And always, always lead with love. The impact you have will ripple through more lives than you will ever know.

1.
Sole, Not Sky

Imagine losing your heart—only to find it in an unexpected place. Imagine redefining your understanding of love and identity through the most personal loss and discovery. That's the journey of transformation and acceptance that this book will take you on. Conceived long before the manuscript's inception, the title, *Sole's Mom,* has a deep significance: it represents my desire to commemorate and honor Sole, my child, whose presence, though brief, left an indelible mark on my life. Since starting this project, I have been asked three recurring questions: Why not *Sky's Mom* instead? Does Sky know about this book and support it? What do I hope to achieve through writing this memoir?

I. SOLE, NOT SKY

Sole's Mom is a fitting title because it is my swan song to Sole, the child I have lost. It is a way for me to pay tribute to Sole's memories and her impact on my life. Additionally, there is a deeper reason for choosing this title, which I will elaborate on later.

To answer the second question, Sky, my other child, who shares a deep bond with Sole, is fully aware of and supportive of my project. He understands the journey I am going through and believes in the importance of our family finding closure. This idea brings me to the third question: What do I gain from writing this book? Firstly, this book is part of my journey to accept the reality of Sole's transition from the daughter I gave birth to and loved deeply to the son they are today. Mothers of transgender children will understand the complex emotions and struggles associated with the revelation of Sole's gender identity.

Society defines gender based on biological differences, specifically the sex chromosomes: XX for females and XY for males. However, scientific research and medical understanding reveal that there can be variations and unique traits that accompany these classifications. You may be wondering: Are these variations mistakes? And if so, when, and where were they made? If you believe in a higher power, did God make the mistake? As the mother and carrier of life, I, too, embraced the misconception that any deviation from traditional gender and chromosomal configurations was erroneous. This irrational guilt and self-questioning are common among mothers of transgender individuals, as expressed in Andrew Solomon's book, *Far From The Tree*.

Nevertheless, I have worked through these emotions and have come to a place of acceptance. Through this book, I seek to reach personal catharsis and offer understanding and support to other mothers on that shared journey toward healing and acceptance. While writing *Sole's Mom*, I achieved closure for the inner conflict I experienced regarding Sole's transition to Sky. Through understanding and documenting my experiences, I hope to provide solace and support to other mothers who may be facing similar challenges with their transgender children.

One of the most significant difficulties in addressing the transgender issue is the use of pronouns. You will find that I toggle between "she/he" and "Sole/Sky." The best solution I found to avoid confusion was to use the feminine from birth to more or less their fifteenth birthday, as till then, she was our Sole. This approach reflects the transition Sole experienced, mirroring the gradual change in identity. In his second year of high school, he officially declared himself a transgender person. It took me a while to accept, understand, and honor this transition, so I still referred to him as Sole, our daughter. This delay in pronoun change is not uncommon among parents of transgender children, highlighting a period of adjustment. And so, in the book's first chapters,

I speak of "Sole." I use the masculine and "Sky" to align with Sole's affirmed identity when relating her high school years. But even then, to give you a sense of the turbulence we were experiencing, there will be mention of Sole, our daughter. This dual reference illustrates our family's evolving understanding of Sole's identity. Please bear with me on this.

I have also stated throughout the book that I am not writing this as an authoritative figure on gender issues. I have not conducted any survey or collected any data on the issue. Over the past few years, I have listened to others' journeys and read interesting books on gender. I listened with fascination to Andrew Solomon as he read from his book *Far From The Tree* at Books and Books in Coral Gables, Florida; he discussed identity as he approached the subject of nature versus nurture. I read Maggie Nelson's *The Argonauts*, where she explores themes of gender, love, and identity. I delved into *And Tango Makes Three* by Justin Richardson and Peter Parnell, which conveys a beautiful message: love is all they need. I watched a documentary, *Of Men and Gods*, by Ann Lescot and Laurence Magloire, that examines the lives of some Haitian men who are gay. I have learned from all those and some others, but in the end, this book retraces the journey of a mother who gave birth to a daughter, Sole—a daughter who, later in life, declared that she was born in the wrong gendered body and became Sky. In sharing my story, I sincerely hope that others going through a similar experience will find something they can use to help them deal with this complex transition.

2.
The Longing for a Daughter

As I delve into our family's story, it's essential to understand our initial longing for a daughter. After three sons, my husband Pantal and I naturally harbored the hope of having a girl—and many others in the family prayed for that miracle as well. Because I was over thirty-five during my fourth pregnancy, the doctor strongly advised me to undergo an amniocentesis. In the context of pregnancy, thirty-five is considered "geriatric," and there are increased risks of chromosomal abnormalities, such as Down syndrome, in babies born to older mothers. Amniocentesis helps identify potential genetic disorders early on, allowing for informed decisions and preparations by expectant parents and healthcare providers.

While performing the procedure, the doctor considered the sonogram and confidently declared, "It's a boy!" A wave of despair engulfed me, an indescribable mix of disappointment, confusion, and unmet expectations.

Interestingly enough, I had never truly desired a daughter before. I always wanted two boys and was content after having my first two sons. However, five years after Antoine's birth, I became pregnant again. Along came our beautiful Kahlil, and with the arrival of this third boy, the consistent refrain I heard from everyone around me was, "When are you going to have the girl? She would be so beautiful, with long, flowing hair." Long hair was—and still is—considered a desirable attribute in Haitian and other black communities. This societal expectation of having a daughter with luxurious, cascading hair reminded me of my mother's experience in Haiti, highlighting how deeply ingrained these ideals are. Because of her Italian heritage, she had long, wavy, beautiful black hair. As a teenager, wanting to feel more mature, she begged her mother for a haircut. Finally, my grandmother relented. When my mother arrived at school, very proud of her "bob," the head nun told her with deep disappointment, "You have removed what made you so charming, your link to the white race." The expectation of having a daughter with long hair, no less, was firmly ingrained in our society.

I often heard parents argue that raising daughters was easier than sons, a notion I began questioning based on my

2. THE LONGING FOR A DAUGHTER

parenting experiences. Daughters are perceived to be softer, more obedient, and more affectionate; there is a consensus on this point. Many mothers also shared with me the idea that only grandchildren from daughters would ever genuinely be close to you, as the bond between a mother and her daughter often transforms into a shared experience of motherhood, enhancing the grandmother's involvement and connection with the grandchildren. This shared journey of motherhood between a mother and her daughter lays the foundation for a richer, more intimate grandmother experience when the daughter herself becomes a mother. With sons, it's not the same. Men traditionally leave the responsibility of childrearing to their spouses, leading children to connect more organically to the maternal side of the family and less so to the paternal side. The concept of grandchildren held a strong allure for us, prompting us to contemplate these notions. We received countless opinions and beliefs from various sources.

Thus, the seed was planted, and we decided to try one more time, praying for a girl. We would keep the baby's gender a surprise until birth, as we had done with our first three children. This idea was Pantal's. For myself, I wasn't thrilled about going through an entire pregnancy without knowing the baby's gender, so I decided to find out and keep it a secret from everyone else. When the doctor announced another boy, my heart sank with disappointment and unspoken grief, a feeling hard to articulate but deeply felt. A sense of frustration washed over me as the doctor and his assistant left the examination room so I could get dressed. A minute later, they suddenly burst back into the room, laughing.

The doctor said, "My assistant here thinks I made a mistake. So let me take another look."

A surge of conflicting emotions rose within me—hope, anxiety, and cautious optimism. With the cool gel on my abdomen again, the examination proceeded, this time a bit slower. A few minutes later, the doctor agreed with the nurse's suggestion that it might be a girl. However, he cautioned me not to rely too heavily on the sonogram as the factual accuracy would come from the result of the amniocentesis, scheduled for two weeks later. Hope filled my heart. A daughter!

Driving away from the clinic, I turned on the cassette player in the car, and the voice of Haitian singer Ti Corn filled the air with "Latibonit," one of her most beautiful songs:

Latibonit, o! Yo voye pale mwen
Yo di m Sole malad
Lè mwen rive, mwen jwenn Sole kouche
Lè mwen rive, mwen jwenn Sole mouri
Se regretan sa pou m antere Sole
Se douloure sa pou n antere Sole

2. THE LONGING FOR A DAUGHTER

My reaction then was that I didn't need more test results or evidence. I was having "my Sole"! It was a certainty that didn't require any scientific proof. It felt like a higher power was speaking to me. Now, I can't help but wonder about the connection between this song and the eventual passing of Sole. My mother had difficulties with the lyrics, as she couldn't move past the idea that it was foretelling Sole's death. However, for the rest of us, it was the melody itself and the words, though sad, that resonated with us. I refused to entertain the thought of a predestined death. Sole, in Creole, is a variation of the word for sun. Therefore, I envisioned Sole to be my sunshine. That was all that mattered.

3.
Choosing the Name

Let me take you back to where it all began—the story behind the name "Sole." In our youth, my husband and I read André Gide's *Les Nourritures Terrestres* (*The Fruits of the Earth*) and were captivated, like many, by this book. Gide dedicates the book to a fictional disciple named "Nathanaël," a name derived from Hebrew, meaning "God has given." He encourages Nathanaël not to settle for mediocrity but to pursue a life filled with adventure and passion. Independently of each other, both Pantal and I had decided if we had a son, he would be named Nathanaël. Pantal, in his first marriage, had two daughters. So, our first child, if a boy, would be Nathanaël. If a girl, we wanted a Haitian name, and the choices were either "Sole" or "Aïda." "Sole" comes from the very soulful Haitian song "Latibonit" and is a bit of a variation of "sun" in Creole. As for "Aïda" (written "Ayida" in Creole), in Haitian culture, it symbolizes the spirit of fertility, rainbows, wind, fire, wealth, thunder, and snakes. The rejection of "Aïda" by the family wasn't just a matter of preference; it reflected deeper cultural nuances and family dynamics, with the understanding that this name was that of a poor peasant with very kinky hair, "Aïda, tèt kwòt" in the Haitian culture. To which I would always reply, there is no way she would be a "tèt kwòt"! Though Sole was not totally accepted either, it was at least tolerated by those who wanted to avoid Aïda. Ultimately, this became a non-issue as, happily, we had a boy. Nathanaël was born.

The two names under consideration for our second child were "Antoine," after my maternal grandfather, and again "Sole." Pantal and I were students at the University of Florida in Gainesville, far from family and friends—I took a semester off to go to Haiti for the birth, to be home with my parents; Pantal stayed in Gainesville to continue his studies. One night, I was home alone with my mother, and I heard her voice in the dining room, repeating the name "Sole" in different tones: "SOle..." "SoLE..." My mother practicing "Sole" with various emphases was more than a rehearsal; it was her way of coming to terms with our unconventional choice, revealing the complex layers of acceptance. Eventually, she'd have to say it in a very upbeat and authoritative tone that didn't allow negative comments!

After all, certain names carry specific connotations and expectations in Haitian culture. She wanted to be ready to face the cultural implications of "Sole." And when a boy was born, she sighed with relief.

The name "Antoine" wasn't without some ambivalence. Before the delivery, my grandmother kept on asking me, "Are you sure it is okay with Pantal?" to which I would always answer, "Yes, Mèmère, he knows, and he loves it." She worried that Pantal might disagree with a name that represented my family alone. When I came home from the hospital, I placed the baby on her lap, saying, "Voici Antoine!" With a beaming smile, she said, "Well, zafè Pantal! This is Antoine!"

Five years later, when I got pregnant again, the third child would surely be a girl: "Sole"! We had a mental block and couldn't even think of any name for a boy. Around that time, Nelson Mandela was at the forefront of the news in South Africa and internationally: he was to be released from prison after twenty-seven years! Mandela's struggle and resolve captivated us, and in a moment of inspiration, Pantal and I considered honoring his legacy in our son's name. Everyone else was against the idea, as "Mandela" was deemed fitting for a last name, not a first. So when I gave birth to a boy again, on his first day with us, he was called "the boy"!

Referring to him as "the boy" reminded me of an incident in Brooklyn, New York, about fifty years ago. I'd just moved to the States and spoke almost no English in the twelfth grade at Wingate High School. The class had to write a book report about Richard Wright's *Black Boy*, which I read with a dictionary in hand. To tell you the truth, I did not understand much about the plot—only that the main character, a boy, was poor and had some troubles. So, in my report, I wrote, "The boy went home. The boy's mother made dinner. The boy was not happy." Then I thought, "This is boring, repeating 'the boy' so many times." Why not change it sometimes to another word in the book that seemed to generate some excitement? So here I went: "The nigger did this." Oh, Lordy! The anger of the teacher when he returned our papers to us! I sat so quietly in my chair, hearing him vent and scream, thinking in the good old Haitian tradition, someone was going to be slapped in the head! I was shocked when he slammed the paper on my desk! Another Haitian classmate explained to me afterward what I had done wrong. To this day, I remember vividly this scene, wishing I could have a talk with this man and ask him what did he think had happened here, as he very obviously knew two things: one, I was also a "nigger," and two, I was new to the country and spoke very little English! Reflecting on this misunderstanding from my past helped me appreciate the nuances and complexities of communication, a theme that resonates in my journey with Sole.

Now, back to "my boy"! As night fell and the hospital grew quiet after my family left, I was fretting: *What am I going to say when they ask me to name him officially?!* At two o'clock in the morning, I called Pantal at home. "We must decide!" I insisted. I still imagine my husband in the wee hours: groggy from a long day of labor, one eye opened; he sees Kahlil Gibran's book on the nightstand, *The Prophet,* and suggests, "Call him Kahlil!" And so, with a mix of spontaneity and destiny, "Kahlil" became his name, marking another chapter in our family's story.

Do you understand then the divine intervention I saw when the song "Sole" started playing so randomly as I left the clinic years later?! And, of course, two weeks after that, my doctor confirmed we were having a girl! I could have told him, "I know." Dr. Ross was a modern-day Dr. Welby, embodying the compassionate and wise characteristics of the beloved television character known for his patient-centered approach and dedication to his community's health and well-being. Knowing that we already had three boys and that I was rooting for a girl this time, he was excited to tell me the good news. At that visit, I found him waiting for me at the door of his clinic. When he saw me arrive, he met me in the parking lot and gave me a great big hug. On the clinic window, a sheet of paper displayed "XX"! My Higher Spirit has a weird sense of humor, no?!

3. CHOOSING THE NAME

With the first three kids, Pantal and I had decided not to find out the babies' gender until birth. But as I said, I couldn't bear the not knowing.

"Maybe we should find out this time," I suggested in the beginning,

"Nope," he said, "let it be a surprise."

So now I knew, but no one else did, not even Pantal. For all my previous pregnancies, he'd always gone with me to my monthly doctor's visits; this time around, I had to find various excuses to keep him from accompanying me, as Dr. Ross would be unable to hold the news from him! My mother kept warning us not to expect a girl too ardently. Pantal's mother reminded us that his uncle had seven boys; maybe we would face a similar situation to his aunt, who kept trying over and over for a girl. So often, I came very close to telling, but I was reluctant to say anything. Only two people knew: my sister, Mildred, and my aunt, Marraine Lala. The former sent me a pretty pink dress for Sole to wear upon leaving the hospital, with an express direction not to open the box before the baby's birth! Marraine Lala gave a pretty pink Quartz stud for the baby. Yes, Sole was expected with joy!

Lately, I've asked myself repeatedly, is there any significance for those two names chosen for this long-awaited girl? "Latibonit o, yo voye pale mwen, yo di m Sole malad, yo di m Sole mouri, se regretan sa pou m antere Sole," a death foretold. "They sent for me to tell me that Sole is sick, Sole has died. Oh, it's hard to bury Sole." Was my mother right in her mistrust of this song? The beauty of these poignant lyrics did not touch her. She just saw the death announcement and rejected it. Both names somehow seemed to carry a projection of the fate of my daughter: Sole, whom we've had to bury, and Aïda, the spirit of the rainbow. What if we had chosen a more traditional name, "Catherine," "Lucie," or "Emilie"? Would we be facing this situation still? Who is to know? We'd carried these choices for over a decade, three pregnancies. Finally, here she'd come, ten years later, and we'd lose this daughter to an unexpected transition.

I don't know that I believe that the choice of the names had anything to do with Sole's life. It was her fate and the fate of the family to deal with this experience. Everyone who's been in contact with Sole/Sky, I believe, has learned a little about love, acceptance, and understanding.

4.
The Early Years: A Different Kind of Girl

"We have a girl!" Oh, the joy! When she was born, the whole family was with me in the birthing room at the hospital. Pantal's joy was overwhelming. The boys were so excited. My mother-in-law was there! So were my brother, who shed a few tears, and his wife. The collective sigh of relief was an outpouring of pent-up emotions, a palpable sense of shared relief and joy. Then, a couple of hours later, the news came. During Sole's first examination, an unexpected turn led to a startling, albeit temporary, concern: the doctors believed Sole was blind! What?! Everyone was stunned. What should have been a moment of unbridled joy turned into collective anxiety, casting a shadow over our initial happiness. There was the coffin in the living room! That was the atmosphere in the room. It was Saturday. We would have to wait till Monday for a specialist to do a more in-depth examination to understand better what was happening. So, instead of going home on Sunday, we were kept till Monday.

Monday, the specialist arrived; he took my Sole away and, after an interminable five minutes, brought her back, saying very casually, "Everything is fine." Her eyes were so black that they couldn't see the back of the pupil with the rudimentary instrument used at first, hence the conclusion that she couldn't see!

The relief! We dressed promptly and took our precious girl home in Mildred's pink dress.

Sole was my live doll! I dressed her mostly in pink and pastel colors. She received dolls from everyone, though strangely, not much from me. Only once did I buy her a doll, and I got it for her because it had a pretty embroidered dress in blue denim, Haitian style. This doll is still the centerpiece in our living room. My husband insists on keeping it and displaying it. I will talk about it again, but for now, I'll say this: I did notice that I was more interested in the dolls than she was. One Christmas, when she was about eight, her cousin from Haiti came to visit. I was pretty happy because Melina was the ultimate "proper" little girl who loved "accessorizing" her dolls! I thought her enthusiasm would be so contagious that Sole would finally be attracted to the dolls and the idea of playing house—as any little girl should be! One day, they were very engrossed in their play, and as I passed in front of the bedroom, I heard Sole tell Melina: "When you leave, I wish you would take all of them with you so that Mom can stop bugging me about playing with them!" She had a begging tone to her voice. Sole's disinterest in traditional "girl" toys was an early sign of her forging her identity. So, there went my dream of a "regular girl" playing with her dolls and girlie toys!

One thought assuaged my worries: This behavior was not unexpected. Sole spent a lot of time with Kahlil, who was very close to her age, and with their good buddies, two young boys who lived across the street from us. Besides, all the young cousins near her age were also boys. It was inevitable—she would prefer boys' activities for now. What did she do most days? She rode her bike, roller skated, and played ball with the boys. At the YMCA, she joined the boys' soccer team. In pre-school, her best friend was a little boy who told everyone he would first marry his big sister, then Sole, when he got older. When she was a pre-teen, a Haitian family moved into our neighborhood. Oh, the joy! They had a daughter just a few months older than Sole. But as much as we tried to get them closer, they never hit it off. Sole had some girlfriends but seemed more drawn to the boys and their activities.

By age six or seven, putting the pretty pink dresses on her was getting more and more challenging. As Sole grew, her resistance to pink dresses symbolized more than a clothing preference; it asserted her emerging sense of self. She preferred to dress in shorts and t-shirts, and I resigned myself most of the time. Her style of play, of course, warranted that. For her fifth birthday, her godmother took her shopping for a cute dress at an exclusive children's clothing store. After looking at what the store had to offer for girls, Sole confessed, "I wouldn't say I like dresses." They settled on a pretty green overall.

In another memorable anecdote, I was on the phone with a cousin, casually talking with her while Sole screamed bloody murder in the background.

Finally, my cousin asked, "What's going on at your house, Isabelle?"

I laughed. "Nathanaël is trying to put a dress on Sole, and she refuses! She has her back to the wall, screaming!"

At that time, I thought it was cute and funny.

Years later, as I struggled with the transition, I asked myself, if I had not given in to her penchant for "boy things," could she have gone a different way?! Why did we let her do soccer and not enroll her in ballet or theater? By allowing her to play soccer, maybe we'd accepted her masculine side too readily, the emerging "Sky" part of her. I wondered whether we should have insisted on her wearing the dresses and denied her the shorts and t-shirts. Not have allowed her to play soccer. In her Girl Scout troop, she was the only one not in dance or gymnastics. She wouldn't hear of it. So I let it go. When I miss Sole, I still wonder: Did I do something wrong? It is the strong point of humans to think of themselves as all-powerful and in control of everything.

In truth, Sole was a happy kid in elementary school. She was very open, affectionate, and obedient. Never a tantrum. She was the girl I was foretold, a soft, docile child with gorgeous long curls. She was very close to her dad. The joke among us was that if Papa was going to hell and I was going to the mall, and we asked Sole, "Who do you want to go with?" without thinking, she'd go, "Papa!" This lighthearted family anecdote, while seemingly trivial, underscored the special bond between Sole and her father, a bond that remained strong even through her transition.

A song we loved to listen to was "À ma fille" by Charles Aznavour. In the Haitian tradition, this is the go-to song at all weddings—the one reserved for the father-daughter dance. We played it often in repeat mode at the house, and I mouthed the words in English as Aznavour sang in French.

> Je sais qu'un jour viendra / I know one day will come
> Car la vie le commande / For life will soon demand
> Ce jour que j'appréhende / This day I fear
> Où tu nous quitteras / When you will leave us

Je sais qu'un jour viendra / I know the day will come
Où triste et solitaire / When sad and all alone
En soutenant ta mère / While holding on to your mother
Et en traînant mes pas / And dragging my steps
Je rentrerai chez nous / I will go back home
Dans un chez nous désert / In a deserted home
Je rentrerai chez nous /I will go back home
Où tu ne seras pas. / Where you will no longer be

And we would fantasize. Pantal would sing it to Sole, and I would dance with her. Oh, how I loved the idea of a wedding! Sometimes, I would secretly practice the steps to the dance with Sole so that we could do it perfectly. Other times, while her papa sang and I danced with her, halfway through, her three brothers would join us on the dance floor! Oh, the sensation we would be!

Do you understand, my Sole, my Sky, that I feel somehow cheated of my dream?

Remember my meltdown the night of your birthday a few days after your top surgery? It was the crashing of all these dreams born when Dr. Ross gave me that big hug in the parking lot, announcing, "It's a girl"!

Isn't it the dream of all parents to know their child is set in a good relationship with a loving companion, with children and a family that will support them in their daily living? I hope you find the one—that person who will be there in good and bad moments, who will hold your hand at the end of life as you leave this earth. Do I wish too much?

Thinking of your friends, Luke, a transman you met at YES, and Karen, his beautiful wife, I see the possibility that you'll meet the person of your choice who will take your heart away.

But I worry about you, my child, my heart.

5.
Middle School Revelations

During middle school, Sole strongly preferred activities traditionally associated with boys, such as soccer. She was never interested in boys except as sports partners, though she was a bit of a sensation in middle school. Sole's unique style was a vibrant expression of her individuality and became her signature in middle school. Every Friday, she demonstrated cultural pride by embracing her Haitian heritage in a personal way that celebrated her roots. Whatever shirt her papa owned with Haitian designs—the Haitian flag, the Citadelle—that's what she wore.

Though she wasn't impressed by the interest the boys were showing, she would enjoy telling us about it occasionally. Once, at a mall, she caught the fancy of a couple of boys who were there with their mother. Not realizing we were also Haitians, they said out loud, "Ou bèl!" "You are pretty!" Sole's reaction to the compliment, a mix of surprise and modest pleasure, hinted at her burgeoning self-awareness. She asked me to recount the story to the family over and over again. She loved it! I hung on dearly to this incident at the beginning of her transition. While I may have embellished the memory, reflecting back, I wonder how Sole truly felt about the attention, beneath the surface of my interpretations. I always assumed that since she thought the encounter had been cute, this meant she "liked boys." Years later, when I reminded Sky of the incident, he didn't remember it at all. Was it all in my head, the pride, the blushing because those guys thought her cute? The lies we weave to appease our hearts.

Reflecting on Haiti's conservative stance on sex education made me realize the challenges Sole might have faced in navigating her own sexual identity in such an environment. Religious beliefs in Catholic communities play a significant role in shaping attitudes toward sex. Catholic education mainly advocates for abstinence-based approaches and opposes comprehensive sex education. Strangely, the thought is, "What you don't know can't hurt you." Experiencing my first menses without support shaped my resolve to be there for Sole, a resolve that was tested as she navigated her path. In my youth, our nanny Marie was the one I'd gone to, and she'd provided the supplies needed to handle this event. Before I started bleeding, there had been no explanation, cautionary words, or preparation for what to expect. Marie eventually told my mother, who ignored the subject and never mentioned it to me. I remember another incident involving my very close cousin, Danielle, who had her period before I did. Once, we were walking in the street, and some guys whistled at us as we passed them. We had the most significant moment of panic, fearing this simple act might get her pregnant. We knew there was some correlation between the two events—a young woman's period and her pregnancy—since you become a woman when you start menstruating and can, therefore, bear a child. What if a guy hollering at her was all that was needed?! How and why a woman became a mother was a mystery. When I became a parent, I promised myself to do much better with my children.

At the beginning of my career as a sixth-grade science teacher at Booker T. Washington, part of the curriculum included Human Growth and Development. Before starting the unit, I sent a letter of intent to the parents, asking them permission to involve their children in the lessons. One mother came to the school to ask me furiously to keep her twelve-year-old daughter "out of this," stating that "this is what puts ideas in a child's mind." Too much knowledge—that was her complaint! I had no other choice: Every day for the following two weeks, I had to send the young lady to

5. MIDDLE SCHOOL REVELATIONS

the library with an alternate assignment. When we returned from Christmas break in January, I found the mother waiting for me in the office. In tears, she told me how sorry she was to have kept her daughter from this unit because, over the break, she'd found out the girl was pregnant.

What is it that makes us shy away from talking openly to our children about sex and sexuality? This question led me to examine my hesitations and the cultural barriers in discussing those important topics, particularly in the context of Sole's journey. I urged parents to speak to their children about the birds and the bees. But despite my firm resolve to be open with Sole, I found myself repeating patterns from my upbringing, struggling to bridge the gap between intention and action. Sadly, I did not do any better than my mother! The day Sole first experienced menstruation, a pivotal moment in her life, coincided with my absence, marking a missed opportunity for maternal support during a significant transition. I was away for a seminar in California, and my sister watched over the family in Miami. Sole had her period without me. Rather than acknowledging to her aunt that something big was happening, she casually asked her older brother to get her the necessary items, which means my sister didn't realize it was a first. Upon my return, I mishandled Sole's nonchalance because I felt guilty for not being there.

In retrospect, I treated it too casually. I should have made a big deal out of it! If I am to be totally truthful, my reluctance to discuss her menstruation openly with her stemmed from my Haitian background and an influential upbringing steeped in secrecy and avoidance. Because of this false start, her period became a sore subject between the two of us moving forward. A friend of mine who had two girls about the same age as Sole would freely discuss their symptoms and needs with them; their conversations were open, and my friend sometimes included Sole and me in them. I missed that so much with Sole; she had her guard up whenever the topic arose. I took it as a rebuke for letting her go through it alone the first time, though not intentionally. Now, I think she was resenting a hurdle that she must resolve. At that point, she knew herself to be a man; therefore, imagining the rest of *his* life with this monthly affair must have been a significant burden. Oh, wow! What an epiphany! For all these years, the thought never dawned on me, but as I write this, it suddenly comes to me that this must have been part of Sole's reluctance to discuss this with me. As a cousin pointed out, writing this book will be cathartic.

Once, cleaning Sole's room, I saw a diary entry on her desk; she expressed how she liked girls. She liked it when they hugged her. She would hold them a little longer than was necessary. She described how it made her Girl Scout friends uncomfortable when she would tell them so. It was shocking to me how clearly she expressed the feelings she had toward her female friends. Honestly, I was stunned. Discovering

5. MIDDLE SCHOOL REVELATIONS

Sole's journal entry was a profound moment that made me confront my preconceptions and fears. I wondered if she'd left the note to shock me. Leaving out the journal could have been an accidental oversight, but there was still the possibility of a subconscious call for a conversation that Sole wasn't ready to initiate verbally. I pretended not to have read it for a while. I hated myself for that lie by omission, but I had no idea how to approach the subject. Then, one day, I asked her about it. She was vague, somehow insinuating that she had exaggerated; it was "just a story." There are none so deaf as those who will not hear! So, I played the ostrich and buried my head in the sand. I let it go.

The most troubling part of the situation is that I always believed myself to be accepting of homosexuality. My passionate defense of LGBTQ+ rights contrasted starkly with the difficulty I faced at first in applying these principles within my own family, particularly with Sole. Not a shadow of a doubt that I had no animosity toward anyone gay. I was involved in a summer program with the American Physiological Society for a few years in Warrenton, Virginia; it involved science educators spending a week at the magnificent Airlie Conference Center to help the teachers develop their curriculum. On the ground was a lake where some of the geese in the movie *Fly Away Home* spent part of the summer. What we learned about the geese was that some of them presented homosexual tendencies, which made me reflect on the natural diversity of sexual orientation, a perspective I later hoped to bring into understanding Sole's journey. The geese would pair up and get very jealous of their partners. It was interesting to see them always with this or that partner, waddling along the lake, and if another goose of the opposite sex wanted to come along, one chased it off vigorously. To me, the concept of same-sex interaction, which exists with these animals, is also applicable to humans. The geese don't have any malice in them. They can't be good or bad. They are not following a code of morality that they would be breaking by being involved with one of the same sex. If, among these animals, there can be this same-sex attraction, it must be a natural occurrence that doesn't preclude morality. Observing the geese's natural behavior reinforced my understanding of sexual diversity, shaping my response to negative attitudes and informing my support for Sole. I rejected the thought that homosexuality must be perverse.

Justin Richardson and Peter Parnell wrote a very moving book titled, *And Tango Makes Three* (2005), in which they recount the true story of Roy and Silo, two male penguins in the Central Park Zoo in New York. The penguins, who lived together, formed a powerful bond and seemed to share a deep desire to lay an egg so they, too, could have their own baby penguin. Of course, that couldn't happen as they were both male. One day, the zookeeper gave them an egg laid by

5. MIDDLE SCHOOL REVELATIONS

another penguin in the zoo. They lay on the egg day and night until a chick finally hatched. No penguin could have more of a parental instinct than these two male penguins. They were extraordinarily nurturing and loving toward Tango.

This panic at the thought of Sole being gay forced me to confront my own hidden biases and fears. While I outwardly advocated for LGBTQ+ rights, why was I so afraid to approach the question with her? A beloved nephew had declared himself homosexual, and my love for him had not changed at all. I loved him and was very proud of him for daring to let himself be known to the whole family as a gay young man. While the Haitian community often holds conservative views on LGBTQ+ issues, it's a spectrum with varying degrees of acceptance and understanding. At the time of this writing, while same-sex sexual activity is not criminalized, no legal provisions recognize same-sex marriages or civil unions. Again, here, Haitian society tends to be very conservative, and religious beliefs and traditional values very much influence our people's positions. Many LGBTQ+ individuals prefer to conceal their sexual orientation or gender identity due to fear of discrimination or harm. Some face threats to their safety. In South Florida, the Haitian community is somewhat of a closed community. The position here is not as severe as in Haiti, but it is still pretty negative and critical, especially with the older community members.

Did all that come into my fear of acknowledging my daughter's homosexuality? I suppose. But I felt like such a hypocrite. Navigating my husband's reluctance to accept a lesbian daughter added another layer of complexity to our family's journey, highlighting the clash between personal beliefs and cultural norms. How difficult was it going to be in the house? Was I using Pantal's unvoiced position against homosexuality as an excuse not to want to accept this situation? I am still not sure, but I know I was deeply affected by the thought of a gay child. When I think genuinely about it, I see the surface idea was there. What do I mean by the "surface idea"? For Sole's first communion, I sewed a beautiful white dress with laces and embroidery—all by hand. Everyone was awed by my handiwork. And in my heart, I thought, "You haven't seen anything yet! I will surpass myself with her wedding dress!" As a chemistry teacher, my students sometimes asked, "When will we learn to make a bomb?" My standard answer: "I have a daughter I want to see walk down the aisle one day. So, no bomb-making for us!" Dreaming of Sole in a wedding dress was natural for me. I later questioned how these expectations aligned with Sole's dreams and identity.

"I know the time will come/ when this stranger with no face will take you from me… / but if he brings you joy/ my heart to him I'll render…" ("À ma fille" by Charles Aznavour)

5. MIDDLE SCHOOL REVELATIONS

I had imagined her walking down the aisle in a breathtaking dress, a young man, her fiancé, waiting for her at the altar. This is how it is to happen. Sole's announcement that she was gay challenged the dreams I had harbored, forcing me to reevaluate them in light of her needs and happiness. At first, disregarding the hardship she must have felt, I only saw my broken dreams. And for the longest time, I did not say a word about her sexuality—not to Pantal, not even to my brother, Boris, about whom I always say, "If you don't want Boris to know something, don't tell me!" I knew their firm stand on the subject of homosexuality at the time: it was unacceptable. It was hard keeping this secret to myself. My fear of Sole facing rejection was twofold: concern for her well-being and a reflection of my uncertainties about societal acceptance.

I mentioned my nephew, who declared himself gay at a young age. Like Sole, Kevin was brilliant in school, graduating third in his class at Killian High School. In her last year of middle school, Sole kept saying she would continue the "Kevin tradition" in high school. We all assumed she meant his academic prowess, which brought us great joy. As middle school ended, a summer evening brought a revelation that would mark a turning point in our understanding of Sole. We were all going to dinner with Pantal on Father's Day when, at the door of the restaurant, Sole stopped me. "What I mean by 'I'm going to continue Kevin's tradition in school' is that I'm gay." Oh, no! Here was my suppressed secret coming out again to the surface. I was stunned!

I protested. "But you told me it was just a made-up story. Which version am I to believe?"

It turned out I shouldn't have disregarded the journal entry.

Dinner was a blur. I kept on looking at Pantal. He was so proud of his children. How would he take this? He would be devastated. I was to leave for a month in Spain the day after. Faced with the dilemma of sharing Sole's revelation with Pantal before leaving, I grappled with guilt and the fear of leaving him to navigate the new reality alone. But was my concern really about him? I pondered: *Do I cancel my trip? Will it make a difference? What will I say is my excuse for canceling? Will I be able to convince her that she is wrong? Is there anything I can say that will make a difference?*

She'd deliberately chosen to make this revelation right before I left. This was 2005—before WhatsApp and the flexibility of international communication—which meant four weeks of more or less silence between us. I felt cornered. Oh, this was not a happy moment for me. *I won't be there when she needs me. But really, needs me for what?* The frame of mind I was in was not a good one. I left.

With time, rather than dwelling on perceived failures, I began to see these moments as opportunities for growth and deeper understanding. But the beginning was heart-wrenching. Through all that, I felt like a hypocrite. "What is your problem, Isabelle?" I'd ask myself.

Long ago, a good friend of my mother's, talking to her about another friend who had a gay son, commented, "Poor Marie, it's like having a coffin in the middle of their living room." The metaphor of a "coffin in the living room" symbolized my fear of societal judgment, overshadowing the more important focus on Sole's well-being. Did others' opinions matter so much to me, or was it mine I was afraid of? The questions my poor Sole raised! Sole's sexuality put everything I stood for in question. Was my declared love and acceptance of Kevin real? Yes, it was. Then why not embrace Sole's revelation? For a dream of a white dress? With time, I understood that I feared society's reaction to her. ("Will she be rejected? How will she surmount this?") According to our dear friend Arielle, with whom I had a long conversation about Sole/Sky while writing the book, I did not give enough credit to this incredibly strong soul of my son. What I heard the most from everyone who spoke about Sole, and later Sky, was the strength of their character. I did not give them enough credit, I guess. The urge to protect our young, I suppose. Also, it wasn't strictly the dream of the white dress. As I mentioned before, isn't that the dream of all parents to see their children well secured in a relationship with another who will be there for them come "vents et marées" (winds and tides)?

"I know the time will come…/when you will find someone…/your eyes will overflow with happiness and tears…/ he will come along with all his boyish charms…/ with promises of love to make your dreams come true…" ("À ma fille" by Charles Aznavour)

Was it still possible for Sole, and later Sky, to find love and companionship? Yes. But I feared it would be painstakingly difficult, and I could barely manage my distress back then. Today, the most important thing for me is still to know that Sky is happy. That goes for all my children. A friend always said, "You are as happy as your least happy child." And that's a fact. While I longed for a crystal ball to see Sole's future, I realized the true journey was in embracing the unknown and supporting her unconditionally. I dreaded the high school years. Would they be kind to her?

In most societies, hair is considered very important. In his poem "La chevelure," Charles Baudelaire writes of a man who falls madly in love with a Lock of Hair. He caresses it, plays with it, and smells it, to the point of insanity. The idea is that hair does not make a woman, but rather, "it is the woman." As I mentioned before, hair is particularly significant within the black community.

At Coral Gables Senior High where I taught, three of my colleagues and I were very close. Two were white Americans, and the other was Afro-Jamaican. We were a very tight

5. MIDDLE SCHOOL REVELATIONS

group. We spent every lunch together discussing every subject affecting our personal lives. We were one another's support for our lives at home and at work. We talked about our cultures, and one of the topics that often arose was hair care. It was interesting to hear about the hair protocol on both sides. Laurice, the Jamaican, and I were in awe that the other two ladies washed their hair every morning and had time to dry it before coming to school. For us, washing hair was a whole production! First, the washing, then the untangling of the mop, the setting, the drying—it was absolutely impossible to go through that process daily, except if we woke up at least two hours before getting ready for school! We had good fun seeing their shocked expression upon hearing that we only washed our hair once a week!

For a couple of years, I enrolled Sole in the child-care class offered to high schoolers. The students learned to be caregivers, minding after the children of the staff and faculty as needed. Seeing Sole's long braids well-coiffed every morning, my friends, the class instructors, often showed amazement and appreciation for what was involved. Sole's hair was very remarkable. Waist-length and very curly, it was not the easiest to comb. She complained. I complained! My cousin sometimes combed Sole's hair in tiny braids, which would last a couple of weeks. That was an excellent respite for the both of us. But she also hated the long hours spent sitting to have this mop of hair combed. So, she started asking for haircuts. History repeating itself! The horror of the whole family! But she insisted relentlessly.

Finally, one day, I took her to the beauty parlor where I used to have my hair done and told them we wanted to cut her hair off completely. Oh, that did not sit well with the ladies at the salon. Everyone got involved: the clients, the workers, and even the owners. "It would be a crime to cut this beautiful hair off." My hairdresser suggested I bring Sole to her weekly, and she would comb her hair in small tight braids, so we didn't have to deal with it daily. I couldn't bear the despair in Sole's eyes at this suggestion; she dreaded the prospect of sitting among all of these women for hours on end. "No, Mom! Please!" she begged. But they wouldn't hear of it. It had become a community decision. I, not wanting to cut my daughter's hair, was about to give in to everyone's pleas when Sole had the most enormous avalanche of tears. Everyone was stunned, and quietly, scissors were pulled out, and out came her hair, to Sole's great relief and everyone else's regrets. The family mostly blamed me for the change, thinking I was just being lazy and did not want to deal with combing her hair. Of course, her hair grew back; she kept it long for a while, but by then, she was in charge of it. No more pretty bows at the end of her ponytail. When she transitioned into Sky, he kept it short for a while and now has it long in dreadlocks.

6.
Turbulence in High School

In her first year of high school, Sole joined the Junior ROTC. No, life was not easy for her. The bullying in the cafeteria left deep emotional scars, making her high school years more tumultuous than they should have been and challenging her self-esteem. She befriended a group of students who were also gay. She got involved with a girl, Julia. One day, she was in a rather loving embrace with her girlfriend in the cafeteria, and the assistant principal reprimanded them for it openly and harshly. This public reprimand was not just an isolated incident but a reflection of the prevailing attitudes in our education system toward LGBTQ+ relationships. Navigating these challenges wasn't easy; Sole grappled with feelings of isolation and misunderstanding, intensifying the struggle to assert her identity. On her laptop, she had a picture of her and Julia kissing as her screen saver. I lived with the fear that her father would see this picture. My fear stemmed from the potential conflict between Sole's emerging identity and her father's traditional views, which could create a rift in our family. It was a microcosm of the broader anxiety of how her father, and by extension, our family, would react to and accept her true self. I feared Pantal finding out and secretly hoped that Sole would "come to her senses" before her papa learned about Julia. I grappled with how to express my hopes for Sole's future without invalidating her identity, a delicate balance between my fears and her needs. In my heart, I was torn between hoping for Sole's happiness in her true identity and yearning for a return to the familiarity and societal acceptance of a traditional path. I hesitated long and searched deep inside of me to see how to phrase the hope that was in me—that she straightened herself out, forgot about the gay thing, became normal again, and wore that white dress down the aisle. But none of these sounded appropriate.

 Was I that fickle? This question led me to confront my own uncertainties. Was "le qu'en dira-t-on" all that mattered to me? Of course not. I wasn't prioritizing societal norms over my child's happiness; her happiness was always number one. I wanted her to be accepted and supported

6. TURBULENCE IN HIGH SCHOOL

by her father, siblings, friends, and family. What weighed on my heart was a deeper fear of the unknown—of what the world would do to her. And in truth, societal harshness toward differences has impacted Sole directly and shaped our family's fears and strategies for navigating a world that often lacks understanding and acceptance.

So I asked her to take down the picture.

Unfortunately, in doing so, I unknowingly sent a message of non-acceptance, which I later realized may have hurt our relationship and her self-expression. Her response was, "But Mom, if it was Antoine and his girlfriend, would it matter?" To which I answered, "But see, he doesn't have a picture of himself and the girl of the moment, so—" I told her that I felt homosexuals usually found it necessary to flaunt their position a little too openly to shock people and to force the world to accept them. In hindsight, I recognize that this statement reflected my own unexamined biases and societal stereotypes rather than a fair representation of LGBTQ+ experiences. She pointed out that maybe because we disagreed with them, we saw their behavior more blatantly, and they had to exaggerate to make themselves heard and be accepted. Though I agreed with her deep inside, I kept on pushing. And when she took the picture down, I was pleased. "Thank goodness," I thought.

But more hurdles would come.

We were invited to our friend's house in Tampa for a birthday. It would be only Sole and me going on the overnight trip. She asked me if her friend Julia could tag along. Her request to bring Julia, laden with implications about their relationship, left me torn between wanting to support her happiness and fearing potential complications Julia's presence could bring. Oh, the heartache! I didn't want to say no because we'd done it before: we'd taken a friend to the party in Tampa. Since Pantal wasn't going, I agreed so as not to create animosity between Sole and me. I gave her a big lecture beforehand on proper behavior. No holding hands, no kissing (oh, no!), no private conversations between just her and Julia. In retrospect, my extensive list of "no's might have felt stifling to Sole and Julia, unintentionally signaling disapproval of their identity. Was I hoping it would discourage her gayness?! This unacknowledged hope for discouragement revealed my struggle to fully embrace Sole's identity, a conflict between my protective instincts and the need to support her authentic self.

So, along came Julia, and the longest two-day weekend started for me. My constant vigilance, though well-intentioned, likely felt oppressive to Sole, possibly hindering her from feeling truly free to be herself even in seemingly safe places. Never a moment of relaxation.

My reluctance to reveal the true nature of Sole's relationship with Julia was rooted in a fear of judgment, not only toward Sole but also toward our family's acceptance and support of her. What would others say? How would they see me? Would they judge Sole? Pity her? I wish I had remembered Dr. Seuss's words: "Be who you are and say what you feel because those who mind don't matter and those who matter don't mind." If I had shared Sole's identity with our friends, their acceptance could have provided additional support, underlying the value of a trusted community. Their love for Sole, for us, did not suffer once they later realized Sole was gay.

No matter, I had the worst weekend ever.

Again, two essential sides of my character were emerging that I could not understand. Reflecting on my past confidence in defying societal norms, I realized how Sole's situation had led me to value others' opinions more, highlighting my deep concern for acceptance in our community. As a teenager back in Haiti, though a bit of an introvert, I was free of peer pressure. I knew who I was and what I wanted from life; it was all that mattered. As a teenager, some saw me as a nerd, and that did not bother me at all. Where was that free-spirited girl now?

My father was a dreamer. He bought a piece of land in a rather commercial area in Port-au-Prince while he was Consul of Haiti in Cuba. He had a grandiose idea of building the most beautiful house on that land. He made a "maquette" for it and showed off his maquette to one and all. After Castro came to power in Cuba, he returned to Haiti and started construction. All was going well until the house's foundation fell in during construction, and all had to be redone. It would have been a catastrophe for anyone else—not for Papa. He quickly found a solution: remove all the soil and build the house underground, like a basement. Oh, he was proud!

But for Haitian society, that didn't fly! A "sous-sol" home?! What a crazy idea! But he saw past the nay-sayers and continued in his new plans. There were some hurdles, yes, and they required that he adapt our home in unconventional ways. Because of the level, water could not be directed down in the main house. What was supposed to be the maid's quarters at street level of the original plan ended up being our bathroom and the kitchen. To circumvent the underground light problem, he added thick glass blocks in the roof to let light come in downstairs. It was all exciting for him. He took us along with him. Boris and I would sit with him under the beautiful almond tree, and he would help us see the new house. Maybe that's why I was so attached to our "sous-sol." These early morning talks and visualization made the "sous-sol" appeal to my heart.

But not everyone got it. My siblings and I were teenagers, and our social life was complicated. Most of our friends couldn't understand our living quarters. This lack of understanding from others manifested in various ways, from awkward questions to outright disapproval, each a reminder

6. TURBULENCE IN HIGH SCHOOL

of the persistent societal barriers to accepting differences from the norm. Where my other siblings minded the "sous-sol," I saw it like my father: very ingenious. "If you have a problem visiting me, then don't," I felt. My father was a great cook, and his paella night was a big hit with many of my friends—at least those who didn't mind going down the basement! And for those who did, it was their loss.

Sole's transition highlighted my latent fears of societal judgment, revealing a protective instinct that overshadowed my previous disregard for public opinion. Well, because it wasn't about me but about my Sole. My intolerable fear of Sole being pitied or judged led me to sometimes overprotective behaviors, struggling to balance my desire to shield her with the need to allow her authentic expression. The idea of the "coffin in my living room" was not acceptable to me at all. Not my beautiful Sole. She was bright, she was beautiful, and she was a lesbian. I actually took pride in knowing she was different from the others. Why wouldn't everybody see that? I was foreseeing a problem that I hadn't even confronted yet. So, that whole first year of high school, it was a taboo subject in the house. I never mentioned anything to Pantal, Sole's siblings, my sisters and brother, or good friends. The only people I spoke to about this were my two cousins, Evna, whose son was gay, and Dannie, who was a breath of fresh air with so much tolerance and positivity. Those two ladies were my rock, my support system in these tough times.

Not long ago, Antoine told me how his friends who had also graduated from Killian would say that Sole was seen in compromising situations with other girls, was in the "gay" crowd and how upset that made him feel. No, Pantal was not the only one struggling with homophobic tendencies in the family. However, with time and open conversations, Antoine would begin to view things differently. He'd start to understand and accept Sole's journey, recognizing the importance of love and acceptance over prejudice. This shift wouldn't happen overnight, but it marked a significant change in our family's dynamics, bringing us closer and making us more supportive of one another's true selves.

Sole's relationship with Julia was a daunting subject to me. Seeing them together, I was ready to bid farewell to the image of Sole dancing in a white dress to Aznavour's "À ma fille." But would Pantal ever be? Would society ever be? My readiness to accept Sole's identity was a significant step. Still, the uncertainty of whether Pantal would reach the same level of acceptance loomed over our family, threatening to create a divide in our united front. Though I know he suspected what was happening, he never said anything, so I didn't either. The atmosphere in the house was not very wholesome. We all knew that Sole was going through "something," but we never mentioned anything. When she wanted to invite some friends over for her birthday (was it her fifteenth or sixteenth?), Pantal agreed after resisting a bit. When it turned

6. TURBULENCE IN HIGH SCHOOL

out that her group of friends were mostly gays and lesbians, my husband was like a caged lion, pacing the patio to see what was going on, but not wanting to appear as if he did not trust them. This situation did not make me happy at all. Despite my yearning for an open, accepting home, I grappled with the reality that Sole's friends, reflecting her journey of self-discovery, weren't always welcomed with the warmth I aspired to offer. Deep down, I wondered: Would it ever go back to "normal"? I wouldn't say I liked that at all. And they certainly felt the unwelcome atmosphere.

7.
Beyond Binaries

Sole was significantly involved with two youth organizations throughout elementary and middle school—the Youth Community of Miami and a youth group at our Catholic church, St John Neumann. At church, she was an altar server and was very involved with the puppet group, which performed everywhere in town and went to competitions statewide. As she entered high school, however, her interest in both groups started to fade. Sole's gradual disengagement was symbolic of the shifts happening within her, and it pained me to see her losing interest in activities she once loved. This detachment was not just from the groups but perhaps a sign of her internal struggle with her identity. She would miss some of her engagements without notifying the team leaders. Understandably, the church removed her from the group. I lamented the way the leaders did it without any conversation with her: they simply emailed her that she was no longer being placed on the schedule. Receiving such an impersonal email was a jarring reminder of how society can dismiss those who don't conform. Sole tried to show no hurt, but deep down, I know it affected her. I offered to talk with the priest, but she said no. It was better this way, she insisted.

She dropped out of the youth group completely. Again, there was no contact with her to find out what was happening. A few years later, an in-depth article was published on social media, recognizing all the youths who had participated in the activities years before; they were already young adults by then, and Sole had become Sky in the meantime. The organization did not mention Sky. His exclusion from the article highlighted a painful reality: society's reluctance to acknowledge and embrace diverse identities, deepening our family's sense of isolation and the struggle for acceptance. When he found out, Sky made one comment: "I guess they can't handle the difference." I'm glad he's resilient; he bounced back, and where I couldn't forget the snub, he held no negative feelings. He is still in contact with one of the kids and never mentioned this to her.

In the spring of ninth grade, there was confirmation time at St John Neumann Catholic Church. Sole had gone through the preparation for two years. As the day approached, she insisted on dressing in pants and a shirt when all girls were required to wear red dresses. Oh, the battle! In the end, I won she wore the red dress. Promptly afterward, she gave the dress away to a friend, a powerful act of defiance, a silent protest against the forced conformity she felt, signaling her discomfort with the traditional female role she was expected to play. By that time, she had more or less disclosed to me that she felt she wasn't a lesbian but rather a man trapped in a woman's body.

At fifteen, Sky declared himself a transgender person.

"Transgender" was a very novel idea to me. As a scientist, to me, you are either female or male. The sex chromosomes say so, XX or XY. There were abnormalities, yes, with Turner syndrome and Klinefelter syndrome being the most common. I tried to call Dr. Ross to see if we could have the DNA analysis from the amniocentesis done for *her* (I was not yet letting go of Sole and accepting Sky). I thought this would shed some light on her orientation. It'd been too long, I was told; no records were kept. Oh, I fought the idea. Where I could deal with her being homosexual, this "transgender" bit was incomprehensible. "You are either a female or a male," I told myself. Yes, you might like "male" activities. Yes, you might enjoy male accouterment. Yes, you might refuse to play with dolls. But how dare you say, "I feel I am a male inside"? Who are you to decide whether you are male or female? All this was beyond me.

7. BEYOND BINARIES

My master's thesis in Science Education was a study on females in science. One of the findings was that up to middle school, girls did better in science than boys because playing with dolls, dressing them, and accessorizing them developed fine motor skills that helped them do better in the sciences—they easily manipulated small instruments and the like. Later in high school, however, because society started praising the boys more in the sciences, there was a gendered shift in interest. For me, Sole's dislike of dolls had little to do with "being a man inside." And her aptitude in science, a field that values inquiry and understanding, simply challenged traditional boundaries. I refused to see it as a reflection of her personal life, her journey of self-discovery.

What was this overwhelming silence surrounding our family? Why was I so afraid of confronting Pantal with Sole's situation? Why didn't I help him through his homophobic beliefs right away? Had I been lying to myself about my open-mindedness? Was it that I, too, felt that there was something intrinsically wrong with homosexuality? Always (always!) I'd proclaim myself free from homosexual prejudice. I had to confront the dissonance between my proclaimed acceptance of homosexuality and my internal struggle with Sole's identity, revealing my own biases and fears that I hadn't fully acknowledged.

I loved my nephew Kevin, and I was happy that he had a very kind partner—a life companion who seemed to love him, and Kevin loved him in return. Still, I was worried about my child. Having a relationship is a tough order for anyone, even with a heterosexual orientation—so many of our friends were single. Adding sexual orientation to the mix makes it even harder to hope for a life partner for Sole. When you also consider the transgender aspect, it becomes even more complicated. Would my child find happiness? How was society going to accept Sky? Previously, where Sole's homosexuality was a concern, the worry was whether she would eventually find someone to make her life with; now, as a transman, how was he going to be received by society?

And there was his father's reaction to his lifestyle. For myself, I was now totally okay with the idea that Sole was a lesbian. I'd grown to like her girlfriend, Julia. It pleased me that my daughter had someone in her life. But a transgender person? I think mothers of transgender children will probably understand my feelings well. To me, you have all the parts of a female being. All the body parts are there, making you a female. But then, what defines a male, and what defines a female? What distinguishes us from each other? I know I am different from my brother, just as I am different from my two sisters. Julia's mother asked me once, "If Sole says she is not a woman but a man, what then does that make Julia? Is she still a lesbian?" This question about Julia's orientation in the context of Sky's identity emphasized the intricate nature of gender and sexuality, urging us to think beyond binary definitions and recognize these concepts' fluidity. I've heard many people ask, "Why couldn't she just be gay?" Suddenly, the complications of being transgender seemed to make homosexuality more attractive.

If you say, "I agree, you are not the declared female you were at birth," this must mean a mistake was made somewhere along the way—a challenging concept. God conceived her through Pantal and me. As I am the one who carried her for nine months as a girl, if now she says she is not a girl but a boy, then it seems I bear significant responsibility for this perceived mistake. Overwhelmed by guilt and shame, I was miserable all the time at first. I took Sky's rejection of Sole personally and felt utterly responsible for whatever misery my Sole, my Sky would have to endure. In the depths of my despair, I sometimes thought, "This means it all started with God. The original error came from Him." And in those moments, it was anger I felt as I resented the idea of a divine mistake. In my turmoil, I struggled to reconcile my faith with the reality of Sole's identity, which led me to question fundamental beliefs about creation and perfection. Oh, these days were harrowing! Andrew Solomon, in his book *Far From The Tree*, recounts the story of a parent with a trans child who received the comment from another parent: "God doesn't make mistakes." She answered, "Look, if God doesn't make mistakes, then your son doesn't have a vision problem and doesn't need glasses. ...it's just a body part.

What's the difference?" Was this comparison valid? Oh, the more I resisted this idea, the more Sole-Sky would stand their ground.

By then, Sky strictly dressed as a boy. More than a style choice, it was a profound assertion of his identity, challenging us to see and accept him as he truly saw himself. He wore a binder for his breasts. Oh! It was painful to see. The binder was on continuously, and Sky removed it only for showers. He endured physical discomfort to gain mental well-being. I sometimes suggested he take it off to sleep, but he wouldn't hear of it. He refused for people to see him with breasts, even his family. My heart broke whenever I saw the vice that bound his upper body; I couldn't hug him, so I wouldn't have to touch it. I could have screamed, "Take this off! It must hurt too much." After all, many people take off their shoes as they enter their homes; I take off my bra. The binding of the breasts bothered me so much. Yet here was Sky, choosing to wear a contraption way worse than a bra. Antoine told me some years later how he tried to put it on once and he couldn't even get it through his head.

Although he kept his hair completely short, despite his efforts, Sky's appearance still didn't fully reflect his male identity—a source of visible distress for him. He had a part-time job at McDonald's, and one day made a mistake in the order of a very obnoxious customer. The man got really annoyed and very loud for everyone to hear; he said:

7. BEYOND BINARIES

"What is this? Is this a 'She-man'?!" and threw his soda at Sky. This derogatory outburst was a painful reminder of the ignorance and insensitivity my child faced, highlighting the societal challenges encountered by transgender individuals. Thankfully, he was well-liked by the management at the restaurant. They got furious at the man and asked him to leave in no uncertain terms. I was so grateful for their support. The supportive stance of the restaurant management provided Sky with a sense of belonging and affirmed the importance of inclusive workplaces.

Sky got involved with the YES Institute in his third year of high school. He met them during a school field trip with the group "Gay Straight Alliance." That meeting was salvation! He started as a casual visitor. He then volunteered with them. After graduating high school, he would be part of their staff for a while. Initially, our family viewed the YES Institute with skepticism, fearing they were reinforcing what we saw as confusion. For us, they were the ones feeding him all this "nonsense" and leading him astray. I didn't understand what he was going through, so I went with him to some of their meetings. I found myself disagreeing with the group perspectives, rooted in my unexamined beliefs and lack of understanding of transgender issues.

Deep inside, though, I was grateful for what they were doing and for allowing him to express his feelings, helping him along. I didn't know what to say, and believe it or not,

I was afraid to let Sky know I was listening so he wouldn't take it as approval. But I listened. And attending the meetings with Sky at the YES Institute turned out to be an eye-opening experience, challenging my preconceived notions and contributing to a gradual shift in my understanding of gender identity. Over time, my family's understanding evolved as we witnessed the Institute's positive impact on Sky. I realized my limitations in supporting Sky, a reflection that prompted me to learn and grow in my role as his ally and parent.

7. BEYOND BINARIES

Instagram cover picture (1997 | 2006)

Wedding in New York, first time dressed as a man, with Kevin, Antoine, and Kahlil (2008)

Sky and Mom. Do you see the love we share? (2010)

High five with Luke at his wedding. Photo by LJ (2012)

7. BEYOND BINARIES

Sole in kindergarten and Sky in Haiti. Same pose, same smile, same heart (2014)

With Fred in Haiti (December 2014)

At Kahlil's wedding. He's the groomsman with his brother Antoine (2017)

On the road to Santiago de Compostela. Sky is being rewarded for good citizenship (2018)

7. BEYOND BINARIES

Sky and his dad. Sky was on his way to Spain to walk the pilgrimage of Santiago (2018)

With Luke and Karen, visiting them in North Carolina (2024)

8.
Challenging More Norms

At one of the meetings, I met a transgender woman who apparently had just changed her name for the third or fourth time. Everyone accepted it; some joked that they wouldn't be able to remember the new name this time around. I wouldn't say I liked that. I thought, "Here is what this whole idea is generating: someone so uncomfortable in their skin, they're constantly changing their personality. This can't be a good thing." I considered saying that out loud but refrained from potentially hurting her feelings. Then, she candidly acknowledged that the name-changing might seem excessive to someone else and said she didn't mind if one forgot her name. She chuckled at herself on that point. Then she got earnest, talking adamantly about the pronoun used to refer to her.

8. CHALLENGING MORE NORMS

She made two points about it. First, it was disrespectful and insensitive on the part of the interlocutor not to make the effort to remember; the emphasis on correct pronoun usage highlights the deep respect and validation it provides, affirming a person's true identity. Then, she insisted on the danger she was placed in if not referred to in the proper pronoun. If someone referred to her as a "he" in a hostile environment, this would put her in harm's way.

I remembered the McDonald's customer and pondered the real-world consequences of misgendering. That incident, where Sky faced public humiliation and aggression, underscored the high risks she highlighted. It was a painful example of how society's ignorance and insensitivity could escalate to outright hostility, reinforcing the importance of respecting and affirming people's true identities for their safety and well-being.

Sky's perseverance in the face of challenges surrounding pronoun usage shows his resolve and growth. Despite the ongoing misunderstandings, he patiently educates our family and friends. Even I have occasionally stumbled over pronouns while writing this book. Throughout the revision process, I've made a concerted effort to ensure that the narrative's shift in pronouns accurately reflects Sky's transition from "she" to "he," mirroring his evolution—and it is not a mistake if I change from "her" to "him" in a single story. If you experience occasional confusion while reading my experience, you can imagine the ambiguity my family was living in.

Initially, in the manuscript, I used "she/her" to honor Sole, wondering when I should start referring to "him," not "her," in the narration. When did Sole transition into Sky? At sixteen? At seventeen? After his top surgery in 2013? I feel there wasn't an exact moment when he transitioned. At some point, for instance, he had yet to change his name. He was still Sole, my son. Only later would he become Sky, a name that held deep personal symbolism, reflecting a continuity with his past and an embrace of his true self, much like the ever-present sun. Up to his fourteenth birthday, every year, I would give Sole, my daughter, her number of years in sunflowers—an intimate tradition we shared. When my child turned thirteen, the florist wouldn't let me purchase thirteen flowers, claiming I could only get bouquets of six, twelve, or eighteen. Only when I explained why I wanted thirteen did he let it go, and I went home with thirteen sunflowers for Sole.

Acknowledging Sky as "my son" was a profound challenge, symbolizing a seismic shift in my understanding and acceptance of his true identity. For the longest time, I would say "my child" rather than acknowledging the transition. At the beginning of my writing, I asked some of our family and friends if the change from "her" to "him" had been difficult for them. The majority said no, focusing on his male appearance for gender recognition.

And those who knew him from the early Sole days say they make the mistake occasionally but move along and correct themselves, encouraged by his nonchalant attitude toward the issue. While others calling him "Sole" doesn't seem to hurt him much, I think the pronoun is more important to him. I guess, like the transwoman from YES highlighted, incorrect pronoun usage isn't just a matter of respect; in specific contexts, it can expose transgender individuals to real danger, both emotionally and physically.

Sky encountered a particularly complex situation, one that would poignantly test his resolve and identity. This incident occurred approximately four to five years after Sky began his transition, name change, and testosterone treatment, which brought about the physiological changes, facial hair, and deep voice, a period marked by both physical and emotional changes. He was upstairs at his aunt's house in Haiti, and she was downstairs with a group of young people who'd come to meet him. He listened as his aunt introduced "her." She talked of her niece from the States, who was spending a few months in Haiti. "Sole will be coming down to meet you soon," she said. She then went on talking of "her" attributes. The whole while, Sky was upstairs, wondering, "What now?" What were going to be their reactions when he showed up? As he recounted the incident, I asked him what he felt about it. Did he consider not going down?!

"No," he said. "Eventually, they will have to know that I'm a transgender person; this way or another, it was all the same."

Sky's pragmatic acceptance of revealing his transgender identity was a brave decision, underlining the ongoing negotiation of privacy and honesty. He was hurt by his aunt's carelessness, but it didn't surprise him as she had never really committed to using the proper pronoun or the name Sky. Many in the family have shown the same inattention (negligence?) in their relationship with him. He insists it's okay. I hurt for him. Some, I feel, are not making a concerted effort to remember. Some family members' struggle with using the correct pronouns stems from ingrained habits and a lack of understanding rather than outright malice or laziness. Their excuse: Oh! That's who I always knew.

Though they remained good friends, he and Julia were no longer dating. He had a good group of friends, and though they were not very welcome at the house, he often hung out with them. By then, Sky's decision to leave the youth group, a space once important to him, was influenced by a growing sense of alienation as he navigated his evolving identity. The altar servers and the puppet groups were all gone from his life. He worked a lot with the YES Institute, and they connected him with an excellent therapist who encouraged us to visit her as a family. The therapy sessions were enlightening, offering us new perspectives on Sky's journey and helping bridge the gap in our understanding and acceptance. And it was the only time we talked as a family about this huge metamorphosis that Sky was going through. I went to a few sessions with Sky. Nathanaël and Kahlil did, too. Pantal and Antoine never. Antoine was the last of his siblings to accept this little brother's existence. Under the exterior of the cool hip guy, he is very old-fashioned and conservative. He admitted to me once that it was hard for him to introduce him as "my brother" to his friends. Eventually, he came around because of his love for him, but still with some reserve.

Once, I saw her alone. The therapist helped me understand that while our support was crucial, Sky's transition was personal, driven by his own needs and identity. When I worried that my acceptance of Sole's choice of clothing, play, and activities when she was little might have pushed her along in this situation, the therapist assured me this had nothing to do with her orientation. She was very emphatic on this point. "Please do not feel you did anything to push him in this direction, nor can you force him to change." At one of our sessions, Kahlil also expressed the thought that maybe he and a cousin, Taro, had been too forward in their acceptance of "Sky" with the other cousins and friends. His view was instrumental in Sky's being so readily accepted as he transitioned. The idea tormented him. He saw Sky as very depressed and mentally ill and feared for the worst.

He'd say often, "I refuse to bury my little brother." There, too, she reinforced the idea that Sky's gender identity was intrinsic, not shaped by external influences or the acceptance of others. If anything, Kahlil had made life more bearable for Sky by helping his cousins and friends accept him. We would always come out a little more accepting and a little more understanding from our sessions with her. Sky says that she played a pivotal role in his life.

A French program I was watching on Le Figaro, "La Fabrique de L'Enfant Transgenre," with Celine Masson and Caroline Eliacheff (February 10, 2023), discussed the influence social media has on young people. "Going through puberty is hard enough," they commented. This program and other narratives shaped my understanding of the complex nature of gender identity. Around that time, I also followed the story of Chloe Cole, a teenager who'd gone through an early transition and was now de-transitioning in her late teens. In an interview with Dr. Jordan B. Peterson, she said, "It is not smart to let kids make permanent decisions during an impermanent time of their lives." During the interview with Chloe, the eighteen-year-old de-transitioner, Dr. Peterson posed the following question, "Would you rather have a live trans child or a dead child?" The prevailing thought on the suicide rate among teenagers is that it is higher among homosexuals and transgender people. Dr. Jordan B. Peterson pointed out—and my research confirmed—that the narrative of heightened suicide rates among gender-diverse youth is more complex, with factors beyond gender identity playing significant roles.

The National Health Service website describes gender dysphoria as "a sense of unease that a person may have because of a mismatch between their biological sex and their gender identity. This sense of unease or dissatisfaction may be so intense it can lead to depression and anxiety and have a harmful impact on daily life." These feelings may lead to suicidal thoughts and medical professionals will try anything to prevent suicide, be it sex reassignment surgery or hormone treatment. Instead of investigating what is at the root of the disorder, they urgently take parents on the path to surgical intervention, which is suddenly seen as perhaps the only recourse. However, there are some horrific stories of young children who went through extensive medical procedures to transition fully at a very early age. Then, a small percentage of them realized their decision at the time was influenced by gender dysphoria. Due to the lack of long-term studies on the subject of gender dysphoria, our knowledge remains limited. However, parents are accustomed to trusting medical professionals. So, when a surgical procedure is suggested as a means to align the individual's physical appearance with their gender identity, a parent might not question this advice.

How incredibly sad. I read some articles and watched a couple of documentaries on young children who thought they were transgender. In their early years, they went through the process of transitioning through sex reassignment surgery, only to realize in their late teens or early twenties that they had made a mistake. They talked of the embarrassment of acknowledging their mistake. They felt guilt and shame at the thought of letting the family down. Their parents had invested time and money in helping them to transition, and now to say, "Oops! I made a mistake." The thought of Sky came to me as I listened to their stories.

At home, the silence was deafening. Pantal would never discuss what was going on with us with anyone. My brother, a significant person in our children's lives, was finding Sky's transition extremely difficult to comprehend and, therefore, accept. For Sky's sixteenth birthday, a turning point in his life, Boris's new partner, embodying generosity and open-mindedness, entered our lives, bringing a fresh perspective to our family dynamic during a time of profound change. She offered to get Sky a present, and Boris insisted on a "pretty dress." Having met Sky, but not fully aware of the situation, she decided on something a bit more neutral than a dress: a skirt and blouse. Sky's jaw dropped when he saw the present. Everyone insisted that he tried it on right then and there. Tight-lipped, he still complied graciously. This is what describes Sky. In this act of compliance, Sky demonstrated a profound love and graciousness toward his family, willing to navigate the discomfort for the sake of familial harmony.

This moment showed Sky's capacity to prioritize the feelings of his loved ones, even when faced with challenges to his own identity.

Our good friend Arielle, with whom I spoke about the book, described Sky as having "the strength to embrace who he is, confident in everyone's love to come out; they don't need to understand to love him enough."

Still, this is one of the moments I will live to regret forever and ever. I do beg you to forgive me, my Sky, for insisting on perpetuating the masquerade.

I was still learning.

In the fall of 2008, a nephew's wedding in New York served as a backdrop for a pivotal moment in Sky's journey, highlighting the family's evolving dynamics and the challenge we faced in embracing his identity. Sky's resolute decision to attend the event in a suit and tie was more than a fashion statement; it was a bold assertion of his identity, challenging us to confront and accept the reality of his transition. "Oh, no!" I said. "No way!" Family members, each with their own opinions and biases, weighed in on Sky's attire decision, turning it into a family-wide debate that underscored our varying levels of acceptance and understanding of his identity. All sorts of suggestions were made, with the most significant compromise being a suit, yes, but a woman's suit. That did not satisfy him. In retrospect, it was a way for him to force the conversation on what he was going through—a way for us to be forced to acknowledge him as a transman. Though the whole family was going to be present at the wedding, Sky said he'd rather not go if he couldn't dress as a man. I agreed with that decision, though disappointed.

Until one afternoon—and that was my first acceptance of his transition—an aunt of mine, Tante Danne, a gentlewoman in her eighties, devout Catholic, extremely religious, put everything in perspective for me in a way I will never forget! Days before the wedding, she said, "Bello, as much as you think you love your child, know that God loves him more." She saw it as if Sky was hurting. And to her, as a Catholic, she says we are not called to judge. We are here to walk with people, listen to them, hear what they are saying, and love them. And that's when, slowly, a shift started happening in me. This woman was remarkable. Her God is all love and acceptance. There is no judgment.

A quick aside to show Tante Danne's character. Pantal was married previously in the Church and then divorced. By getting married in a civil court, we are technically living in sin in the eyes of the Church since he cannot be married in the Church again. Therefore, I am not supposed to take communion. Tante Danne is one of the few Catholics who says, "It is between you and God. If you talk to Him and pray fervently, asking Him for acceptance, you should be able to take communion without offending God."

Sky got to wear his suit and tie. Everyone was present. No one even noticed, and those who did notice didn't care one way or another. We were just very delighted to be all together.

9.
Senior Year

Sole's senior year was fraught with emotional turmoil, identity struggles, and pivotal decisions, each moment laden with the weight of impending adulthood and the complexities of his transition. Again, I have to admit I wasn't there for him. The confusion that enveloped us stemmed from various sources: Sole's evolving identity, our family's struggle to understand, and the societal norms that seemed at odds with our reality. Sole's involvement with the YES Institute ranged from participating in workshops to volunteering for community outreach programs, providing him with a supportive space to explore and express his identity. They provided Sole more than just a safe space; their staff offered tailored guidance, empathetic listening, and affirming validation that bolstered his confidence. The friendships Sole forged at the Institute were more than mere social connections; they were lifelines that provided him with understanding, camaraderie, and a sense of belonging crucial during this transformative period.

In the spring of 2009, a culmination of internal struggles and external pressures overwhelmed Sole, and one day, he decided he wanted to end his life. The pervasive silence at home regarding his transition and the looming uncertainty about his future post-high school significantly contributed to Sole's distress. He grappled with his friends' limited understanding of his transition, feeling a sense of isolation even among those closest to him. This recurring question, "Why not just be a lesbian?" reflects a common misunderstanding, failing to recognize that gender identity is an intrinsic part of a person, not a choice of preference. It reveals how societal attitudes often view being gay or lesbian as somehow more acceptable or understandable than being transgender, highlighting deep-rooted biases and misconceptions.

Sky was still "Sole" to me back then—I refused to acknowledge Sky. And after a heated discussion with a friend, during which Sole unsuccessfully tried to explain herself, Sole took a handful of pills. That afternoon, she was not well. Head spinning, she lost her balance. We went to the doctor, who couldn't see anything wrong with her. She asked us to observe her at home for a day or so. At two o'clock in the morning, I got a distressing text from my child in the next bedroom, telling me she wasn't well, and I needed to come to her. That's when she confessed what she had done. Oh, the despair! Immediately, we went to the hospital, where Sole was "Baker Acted" for seventy-two hours, which means that she was involuntarily admitted for psychiatric evaluation, a legal measure in our state for those in acute mental health crises. As soon as we settled in a room, a young woman arrived and explained that she'd been assigned as a constant observer to ensure Sole's safety. It was very unnerving having someone constantly watch us. That night was a true nightmare. It forced us into a conversation we'd been highly reluctant to have; Sole-Sky's identity was suddenly at the forefront of our lives.

 A charming psychiatrist came to talk to Sole and pointed out that being a tomboy does not make one a boy. She loved all the boys' activities growing up, including playing soccer, but later in life, she met a fellow, fell in love, got married, and now had a wonderful little girl. Oh, I liked her a lot. I preferred this talk much more than what Sole's previous therapist was telling her: that it was okay for her to feel she was a boy. Her perspective added depth to my contemplation about gender fluidity and its challenges. So many thoughts were going through my mind at the beginning of Sole's transition, and I struggled with the concept of gender. I realized that all we know about the other sex is stereotypes.

9. SENIOR YEAR

Traditionally, girls like to play with dolls, and boys like sports. I reflected, "Even if a boy likes pink and prefers to play with dolls, he is not a girl. Sole liking to play soccer doesn't make her a boy." This led me to question: Did that make her a lesbian? A transgender person? Not according to the hospital psychiatrist.

I latched on to her and wanted to know if she could see Sole outside of the hospital when she left. Unfortunately, she wasn't seeing any private patients. As I connected more and more with that therapist's point of view, Sole was feeling more and more distraught. She closed off entirely and wouldn't talk with that woman. Later that day, my daughter was transferred to Miami Children's Hospital, and to Sole's relief, that was the end of our connection with the staff psychiatrist.

In the new hospital, the protocol was rigorous and visiting hours were rigid, which added another layer of stress to an already difficult situation. Sole panicked: She didn't want me to leave her there. But the Baker Act did not leave the decision to me. She ended up staying two weeks at the hospital, and even then, it was against doctors' advice that we took her out.

The immediate visit from the YES Institute's director underscored their commitment to *Sky*'s well-being, offering support beyond their usual educational and advocacy roles. A few of the staff came also. According to their webpage, the mission of this organization is "to prevent suicide and ensure the healthy development of all youth through powerful communication and education on gender and orientation." I remembered Dr. Peterson's question: "Would you rather have a lived trans child or a dead child?" In no uncertain terms, in the hospital, we were confronted with this harrowing choice. We grappled with a maelstrom of emotions, torn between Sky's safety and confusion about the right course of action. And as I interacted with the program director, Martha Fugate, I sensed that the YES Institute's concern was genuine; there was no doubt. Her visits provided comfort and guidance, offering Sky validation and understanding, which was crucial during this tumultuous period. There was no judgment. The promise was that they were there, and he should always reach out to them first if such thoughts came to him. Another staff member who came pretty often was a young transgender man, Luke, for whom Sky had great affection. Sky formed a deep bond with him, finding solace and understanding in someone who had navigated a similar path. Though I was still attached to Sole, I liked Luke's acceptance of "Sky." He was a breath of fresh air every time he visited Sky. He believed in him and showed no sense of judgment. Kahlil's opinion of Luke is that he was the angel that pulled Sky out of killing himself. I started to appreciate "Sky," albeit slowly.

9. SENIOR YEAR

More than the classes and workshops in which I participated, these interactions with Institute members helped me appreciate their presence in Sole's life much better. To be honest, in the beginning, I did not appreciate the Institute at all. I initially harbored suspicions about the YES Institute's influence, fearing they were pushing Sole toward a path that wasn't her own. Sole was in such awe of them that there wasn't much we could have said for her to hear us. Right away at the Institute, it was "Sky/he/him," a young man, no question. One could see a visible sense of relief and belonging in him, something that was painfully absent elsewhere. If Martha, Luke, Joseph, Umut, or any of the staff read this book, they might understand why I sometimes refer to my son as Sole/she/her. They interact with many parents, and they'll undoubtedly get it: up until that time, though Sky had declared himself to be transgender, it was still not accepted in the family. We were still trying to come to terms with Sole's homosexuality, and in the first two years, we did not fully comprehend the idea of a transgender. Okay, Sole didn't like dolls, didn't want to dress as a girl, and preferred soccer to ballet. She wouldn't be caught dead in a pink outfit. Yet Antoine, her older brother, who was a bit of a Don Juan, looked dashing in a pink shirt, and wore it with flair. In my view, it was not reality that had to change but her perception of reality that had to change.

In the beginning, I felt threatened by the presence of YES in Sole's life because I saw them reinforcing her erroneous ideas. My concern was not the acceptance itself but the speed of it; I feared it might support Sole's decisions before she had fully explored them. I was afraid their readiness to accept "Sky" would add more confusion for her. For Sole, this crucial juncture in her teenage years was not just about typical adolescent uncertainty but about grappling with profound questions of identity and belonging. These profound additional psychological problems could create some great turmoil inside. Were we addressing the turmoil by calling my daughter "Sky"?

I'm not going to claim to be an expert on transgenderism. As I share our story, it's important to remember that I am just a mom navigating through unfamiliar waters, trying to work out how best I can to understand my child and help him make a very tough transition in his life. I am hoping to offer insight to others in similar situations. Through sharing our journey, if I can provide even a small measure of understanding or comfort to other families navigating similar challenges, our story will serve a greater purpose. My goal is to foster empathy and understanding, to bridge the gap of confusion and judgment that often surrounds families dealing with gender identity issues. While statistics can provide valuable insights, my focus here is on our journey's personal, human side, which numbers alone cannot fully capture. Yes, we've had to deal with this deep despair that made our Sole want to turn off this bright light that she's given off from birth. And if it means acknowledging that our Sole is gone and now a young man has been introduced into our lives, I am in.

Losing Sole has required a profound emotional adjustment, a process of grieving and acceptance intertwined. And if the name "Sole," our sunshine, is no more, Sky will be our bright moon. Sky's journey signifies a transformation within our family, a new phase where light persists in a different form. He chose his new name well.

Oh! Those two weeks in the hospital were harrowing, filled with moments of uncertainty, long nights of worry, and the stark reality of mental health challenges. Balancing work commitments with strict visiting hours and emotionally draining meetings with the psychiatrist was a relentless challenge, each day a test of our resilience and endurance. The silence permeated our home, a heavy tension over us, stifling conversation and deepening the sense of isolation. Another one of my goals in sharing our experience of having a transgender child is in the hope I can encourage families out there to keep loving their child and accept them even without understanding. It's crucial to understand that the silence at home wasn't a reflection of diminished love but a manifestation of our struggle to understand Sky's experience.

Throughout this journey, a recurring theme played in my mind, echoing my confusion and quest for understanding:

What does it mean to be a man or a woman? I often wondered, "What do you mean you are not a woman? How do you know what a man is feeling?" Returning to the basics of chromosomes, XX, XY, I realized that gender identity encompasses more than just genetic markers; it's a complex interplay of biology, identity, and culture. Let's look at body parts. Breasts, check! Uterus, check! Vagina, check! Large hips, check! Menses, check!... You've got all that. You must be a woman! But although Sky had the typical markers of a female, I began to understand that gender identity is not solely dictated by physical attributes. But we didn't stop there. You can't. I realized that our love for Sky didn't require complete comprehension; love transcends understanding, offering unconditional support regardless of our grasp of his experiences.

The extended family's silence was not just a lack of words but a palpable absence of support, leaving us to navigate these turbulent waters alone. The only person we saw regularly at the hospital was my brother, who made all the family meetings proposed by the psychiatrist. But though he was not ready to accept Sky's transition, he was wholeheartedly willing to walk with us. How I appreciate him in my life! The rest of the family that lived in Miami was absent. My mother-in-law, whom we never saw both at the hospital or at home, called me one day distraught, explaining she realized she should have been by my side during this challenging time,

9. SENIOR YEAR

but she didn't drive and couldn't find anyone to take her to us. I sincerely appreciated the call. But it confirmed that the rest of the family did not want to visit or be with us.

Friends were silent, too. I spoke with friends and neighbors about the suicidal attempt and the hospital stay. Since many of them had teenage girls and boys like Sky and Kahlil, I asked them, "You'll tell the kids, right?" They invariably responded, "I think it's best I don't say anything."

Years later, Mr. Andrew Solomon (*Far from the Tree*, 2015) made me see things from a different angle. More cathartic discovery! It gave me a probable explanation for the silence. He stated, "As the noted psychoanalyst Richard C. Friedman once joked, 'It might help if they all wore t-shirts that said, *Don't worry – it won't happen to you*'" (p. 599). As Mr. Solomon suggests in his book, it is unfortunate the term sex is used "to refer both to gender and carnal acts" (p. 600). It gives them a sense of immorality and depravity to be identified as trans. Is this what was happening? Not to judge anyone, but it was hard. The look in Sky's eyes and his expectation that the other family members would visit every time we saw him were heart-wrenching. Oh, the relief when I told him about his grandmother's call! I could see it in his eyes: "So she loves me?!" Yes, my Sky, she does and is with you and me every step of the way and every day.

My sister was on an international trip then and came through Miami on her way back to Haiti. Her overnight stay coincided with Sky's last night in the hospital. When she heard the news of his attempted suicide, she immediately changed her return date to Haiti so she could be with us all for a couple of days. We went to the hospital to pick him up the next day. That evening, some family members came to visit—it was a very strained visit as it was our first time seeing them since the hospitalization. Sky asked to borrow our car so he could visit a friend from the church youth group who was going through a hard time. Wisely or not, we let him go, out of fear of confrontation and not wanting to disappoint him. Laurence thought it was unwise to let him go out alone so soon after his release, and of course, she was right. She voiced that opinion timidly, but still, Pantal had a terrible outburst at her intervention. Oh, it was not very pleasant! Everyone stayed quiet. No one said a word, myself included. I felt horrible and mortified for her. Here she was, showing concern for Sky and being chastened in front of the others. But where there is love, there is forgiveness. When I tried apologizing to her a bit later, she stopped me and said that wasn't necessary. Pantal's fear and the pressure he must have been going through lately excused any poor comportment on his part.

In these moments, it was clear that love is the anchor in life's storms, a force that binds and heals even in the most challenging times. You don't understand, but you love, and you forgive. I wish this for all transgender people out there.

Again, suppose I touch one or two families going through this hard-to-fathom experience with a family member or a friend. In that case, I will be glad. Reflecting on our story reminds me of a visit years after graduation, when I returned to my high school and sought advice from my chemistry teacher. When I told him I also wanted to teach chemistry, he gave me this advice: "Remember, Isabelle, if you touch one student a year, you have done a great job." I often wonder what my teacher, affectionately known as "Ti St Louis," would think of my efforts now, given this impactful advice during my formative years. Will my words touch one or two?

High school concluded for Sky without fanfare, a quiet end marked by introspection rather than celebration, reflecting his internal struggles during that period. Throughout the year, I repeatedly inquired about Sky's plans post-graduation, but his reluctance to discuss the future seemed rooted in uncertainty and the weight of his transition. Sky failed to attend the SAT, despite registering twice, and his behavior hinted at a more profound ambivalence or anxiety about stepping into the next phase of his life. This is a child who, in elementary school, was voted most likely to succeed. He had great admiration for his pediatrician. He always declared he wanted to be a doctor, a pediatrician. In high school, he was turned on to video making and would waver between medicine and filmmaking. In the summer of 11th grade, he did a summer camp with The New York Film

Academy. That was it—filmmaking! Graduation came and went, with no college in view. We were highly disappointed. But nothing we said would make him change his mind.

In August 2009, I received a fellowship to teach chemistry in India for the next semester. So after the summer, I would be gone, and he would be alone with his dad. He was working at McDonald's. He was eighteen. Unbeknownst to us, he started taking the hormones for his transition. And slowly, he began to change. Upon my return from India in January 2010, the sight of Sky, now visibly altered by hormone therapy, struck me with a complex mix of shock, adjustment, and a deep sense of realization of his commitment to his identity. The shock of seeing Sky's emerging beard was quickly replaced by a swirl of emotions—surprise, a touch of sadness for the child I knew, and a growing acceptance of his new identity. It wasn't much, but the fuzz was there to remind us. Seeing Sky's bearded face was a visual reminder of how much had changed, each glance a confrontation with the reality of his transition and my process of coming to terms with it.

10.
Giving Ourselves Time

Our continued silence was a heavy blanket that smothered our family's ability to connect during this crucial period. When I returned from India, Sky and his brother, Kahlil, decided to move to Orlando—a move that marked a new chapter, not just for them but for us as a family grappling with distance and change. We went with them to help them settle. They were both accepted at the Community College in Orlando. That was a good thing, we felt. Sky spent a semester at the college and dropped out. My disappointment about his academic choices was hard to conceal, rooted in my values as an educator. It created an undercurrent of tension, an unspoken yet palpable barrier in our conversations. I met his elementary school music teacher a few years after high school, who asked about Sole. Her disappointment to know he was working at McDonald's was palpable. It mirrored our society's narrow definitions of success.

But Sky's decisions weren't taken lightly. He wrestled with feelings of uncertainty and disappointment, a struggle we unfortunately didn't fully understand. His stay in Orlando was not very productive. The frequent journeys back to Miami for his hormone treatments were draining for Sky, both emotionally and physically, highlighting the ongoing challenges of his transition. This is the one time in his transition I believe he would have wanted some support from us, from me. But I struggled to find the words to bridge the growing gap between us, to assure him that my love was unwavering despite the tumultuous changes. I could not describe my feelings to the young man before me. Though words often failed me, I hoped my actions—being there for visits to the therapist, preparing his favorite meals (a seafood lasagna would often be waiting for him when coming to town), or simply listening—conveyed the depth of my love.

In defense of homosexuality, I've always believed that life must be incredibly complex and fraught with challenges for someone who is markedly different, living a truth that, while we may not fully understand, is undeniably their own. Instead of understanding that it was Sky's valiant effort to cope with the transition that caused him not to be able to concentrate on school, I blamed his dropping out of school on this turmoil he was going through, a struggle we, unfortunately, failed to recognize and support adequately. As educators, his father and I were genuinely disappointed that he had decided not to pursue a higher education. It felt like the biggest failure.

The reflective conversations I have with myself now, although tinged with regret, are far from useless. They represent a crucial part of my journey toward understanding and accepting Sky's transformation. I wonder if a different approach during his school years, one focused on open communication and support for his identity, might have helped Sky navigate his academic and personal challenges more effectively. What if we'd started asking questions instead of pretending that everything was fine? If we had embraced open communication and asked about his experiences and feelings, we could have fostered a more supportive environment during his transition.

Tell us what hormone treatment is like.
Tell us about your friends and your social life.
Can I ask you if you're happy, or is it a bit far-fetched to talk about happiness, a too mundane feeling?
What are your wishes and dreams?
How do you feel when the world seems to reject you, when the world doesn't recognize you for who you are, when you are called "Sole" instead of "Sky," "she" instead of "he"?

Understanding Sky's emotional well-being could have brought us closer and provided him with the needed support. I often pondered how Sky felt being unrecognized by the world. Later, through conversations and shared moments, I began to comprehend the depth of his resilience and the pain of being unseen. Each hug, where I hesitated at the unfamiliar brush of his beard against my cheek, left me wondering if he sensed my internal struggle to reconcile with his changing identity.

Do you understand, Sky, that my hesitation in our hugs was not a lack of love but an unspoken struggle with accepting the physical changes you were undergoing?
My Sky, was the love I professed enough?

Some of you have asked, "Why write this book? What are you expecting to get out of it?" Here's my answer: I want to understand this transformation that my child went through and come to terms with how I failed him. I also want to recognize how he survived it with brilliance. What a strong character he has, this young man. Sky's strength of character was evident in many ways, such as how he faced challenges head-on and always remained true to himself, even when it was difficult. Our friend Arielle said, "The key is not to dwell on it. Accept, correct the mistake, and move on. Give yourself the grace to grow and embrace Sky's journey alongside him."

10. GIVING OURSELVES TIME

At his book reading at Books & Books a few years back, I told Andrew Solomon about Sky. He signed a copy of *Far from the Tree* to me and wrote, "To Isabelle: Give yourself time." I did. This journey of acceptance was gradual and complex. Each day, I find myself embracing more of Sky's presence, learning to appreciate the unique and wonderful person he is.

When Sky first mentioned the idea of top surgery, I was stunned and overwhelmed with a mix of confusion and fear. He was then twenty-one. Not long before that, we had just lost a very dear cousin, Evna, to breast cancer. First, she lost a breast because the tumor was localized in only that one. Then, barely four months later, the disease reared its ugly head in the other breast, and she had to go through surgery again. Scarcely three months later, she lost the battle to cancer. And here was Sky, expressing a desire to undergo a profound physical change, challenging my understanding of the child I gave birth to and their identity. In our first conversation about surgery, my tone was more confrontational than understanding, creating tension and widening the emotional gap between us. Evna's loss, still a fresh wound, clouded my ability to understand Sky's desire for mastectomy. In my grief, the idea of voluntarily losing a healthy part of oneself was incomprehensible. I had always understood a mastectomy as a medical procedure that is done when you have a cancer that needs to be removed for you to live. It took time for me to recognize its profound significance in gender affirmation for transgender individuals like Sky.

I wondered: If you lose your breasts and become a man, will you love differently? Will you care differently about your fellow human beings? Will you eat differently? Will your physical and emotional needs be different—better?

The mastectomy certainly didn't help Evna; we lost her beautiful presence in our lives. And that was too close and heart-wrenching to help me understand and accept this next step in Sky's transition. In fact, the shadow of breast cancer in our circle inevitably colored everyone's perception of Sky's mastectomy. Where others fought to keep their breasts, Sky's choice seemed to defy the instinct for preservation. When I mentioned the idea of the book to one of my sisters, she didn't show much interest in participating. Her connection was really with Sole, so she wasn't entirely enthused about the idea of Sole becoming Sky. Not living in the States, she hasn't had much contact with Sky since the transition. About the time Sky was considering the mastectomy, a dear friend of hers was at the same time losing her battle with breast cancer after a double mastectomy. My sister couldn't understand Sky's desire for top surgery.

"I understand her position," Sky said. "I hope she will understand mine one day."

I expressed to Sky my difficulty in understanding why someone would choose to surgically alter a healthy body as part of their journey to authenticity. Another one was losing the same body part in a fight for her life. Coincidentally, as Sky prepared for his surgery, a childhood friend was battling breast cancer, presenting a stark contrast in the reasons and emotions surrounding such medical procedures.

I mentioned my hesitation when we hugged, the touch of the beard against my cheeks. What about the binder he'd been wearing all these years? Every time I felt the tight binder encasing his chest, a symbol of his inner turmoil, my heart sank with a mix of empathy and sadness. So many times, I wanted to exhort him not to wear this horrible contraption. But the code of silence, born out of uncertainty and fear of saying the wrong thing, overshadowed our desire to express support and understanding. Talking about it would be acknowledging the situation. His daily routine of wearing the binder, a constant physical reminder of the disparity between his body and identity, was both a coping mechanism and a source of discomfort. So when he started talking about mastectomy, in the back of my mind, I was seeing the end of this nightmare. That was the beginning of acceptance of this route he was about to take.

Erin Snyder, a very good friend of Sky who has been very supportive of him in all his struggles, with the help of some other friends, organized a fundraiser to help pay for the surgery. He sent us an invitation to the event. My first response to him was, "I gave birth to you once and did it well,

I believe. I have no intention of being part of the birth of this new you." A priori, both his father and I said, "Absolutely not." Up until the last minute, though, I was torn between the fear of losing the child I knew and the growing realization that supporting his transition was vital for his happiness and well-being. Pantal didn't even want to discuss it. But as the event date approached, I realized I had to be there.

11.
Confronting and Accepting Change

I wrestled with my emotions and fears, ultimately realizing that my presence would signify more than acceptance—it would be an act of unconditional love. I was done with the silence. Evna lost her boobs in order to live. My child was going to lose his in order to live a healthier, more fulfilled life. So, I went.

I had the strangest feeling, driving to the fundraiser. I was crossing a significant threshold, taking a huge step that carried the weight of shifting from mere tolerance to active support and recognition of Sky's identity. There would be no turning back on this one. Understanding that Sky's journey was his own, independent of my approval, was liberating yet humbling. My open acceptance of the event was as much for him as it was a crucial step in my journey toward unconditional love and support. Attending the fundraiser symbolized more than just my physical presence, it was an emotional declaration of my readiness to fully embrace Sky with the same love and acceptance I'd had for Sole. It was liberating, but at the same time, oh, so intimidating! I was freeing myself from the chains of denial yet stepping into a realm of the unknown. Again, I still couldn't help the feeling that my acceptance was pushing him toward error. Looking back, I see that accepting his rejection of stereotypical girl attire wasn't about encouraging a "tomboyish attitude" but respecting his authentic self. And I wanted Sky to be authentic. Besides, long before, Sole's first therapist had explained that we cannot make someone transgender by supporting them in their feelings. Denying our daughter the acceptance sought back then would not have straightened her out!

    I knew I had to be there for my son. By attending the fundraiser, I was affirming Sky's identity and acknowledging his journey toward living as his authentic self. And when I got to the event, when his friend recognized who I was, they were all very excited. Everyone stood around, waiting for Sky to acknowledge my presence. The relief and unspoken gratitude in Sky's eyes during our embrace spoke volumes, melting away years of accumulated misunderstandings. It

11. CONFRONTING AND ACCEPTING CHANGE

was all worth it. That moment marked a pivotal turn in my journey of acceptance, where Sole's identity as Sky became fully real and undeniable to me.

This is my son. That's what I told the world that day. This extraordinary person is my son. I believe in him. I think the world of him. And he's strong—willing to go through this operation to liberate himself and ascertain himself as the man he was born to be. My son. My Sky.

Everyone present only had great things to say about him. I saw genuine admiration in people's eyes when they spoke of Sky. "He's an inspiration," one guest remarked, while another shared, "Sky's courage has changed lives." There was a couple with their transgender son who told me their son is alive today because of Sky. The support he showed him during his transition helped him tremendously.

On April 2nd, 2013, he underwent his top surgery, a significant step in his transition. This day is etched deeply in my heart because this is the day Sky was birthed without me.

I understood his excitement. I was happy for him, too, though I felt left behind.

A few days later, we celebrated his 22nd birthday at our home, surrounded by his friends and our family. During this celebration, I experienced a major meltdown.

Everyone was flabbergasted. "What happened?"

I was struck by the realization that my long-held dream, inspired by the song "À ma Fille"—that dream of seeing my daughter in a traditional wedding dress—was irrevocably altered. There would be no white dress and long veil, no Pantal singing while I danced with her. The white dress, for me, was more than a garment for a wedding day. It symbolized a future filled with love, companionship, and societal acceptance—a future I feared might be out of reach for Sky. I worried about Sky being alone in life after I left this earth. I wondered if he'd ever find that one special person to support him through life's highs and lows, rain or shine—someone who would love him and fill his life with laughter and joyous tears. I mourned the children he would never have.

Arielle, who is married to the perfect companion, the perfect soul mate, questioned my sadness over Sky's potential childlessness. She wondered whether I considered her own life incomplete because she and her partner chose not to have children. No, dear Arielle, your life with Sean is the most complete I can imagine. It's not about "the children" per se. It's about the companion who makes having children possible. Oh, I understand that it is still possible for him to meet his soul mate. But for a transgender person, the odds of that happening are narrower. When a friend loses a family member, my saying to them is always, "Hang on tight to your family to help you cope with loss." I know he'll have his siblings and his friends. And if he doesn't find a soulmate, they must be enough.

After his top surgery, Sky's sense of relief was palpable and transformative. One could sense the joy in his life. The family's acceptance could also be felt. We still didn't talk too openly about it, but in one-on-one situations, I acknowledged and discussed Sky's transition and identity openly. Most family members were open to discussing it, with conversations ranging from curious inquiries to expressions of support and understanding.

My husband was now ready to call him "Sky." At a wedding, someone asked Pantal, "Where is your daughter, Sole?" with Sky standing right there with us. Pantal replied with a casual yet firm acceptance, "That's Sole, who is now known as Sky." His response left the person baffled. In another instance, at home, a guest who was very familiar with Sole asked me what had happened to her and whether she had moved away. I answered, "No, he is in the kitchen. He was just here with us. He is a transgender person and is now called Sky." After the initial shock, she remarked on the matter-of-fact way I'd answered her and complimented me on the way I seemed to have accepted such a complex situation. Little by little, Sky was finding his rightful place in the family, not just as a member but as a beloved son fully embraced for who he was.

Sky created a photo collage for his birthday that year. Done artfully, it reminded us of our evolving relationships and the enduring bonds we shared despite the changes. I decided to share it with the family at large and with our friends to officially let everyone know of his transition. Here's the note that accompanied the photo:

"To those of you who were not aware of this, Sole declared herself a transgender person about five years ago. This past week, he has made the change physiologically (is there such a word?!). It's official and legal! Those have been tough times for us. But we are coping. One day at a time. Some days are harder than others. For Kahlil's birth, we used Kahlil Gibran's poem from *The Prophet* as his birth announcement:

> *Your children are not your children.*
> *They are the sons and daughters of Life's longing for itself.*
> *They come through you but not for you...*

Talk about a prophecy! I wanted to make you aware of this, my family, my friends, because I figured it might confuse you when you see our family photo. We are still very new at the new him/he/son appellation. But we are trying. I tell Sky, 'petit à petit.' We'll get there."

Everyone's response was very positive.

In the fall of 2014, he went to Haiti for a few months, hoping to establish himself there. His decision to move to Haiti, a search for roots and identity, filled me with pride and apprehension. His courage to face a society known for its intolerance spoke volumes of his growing self-assurance.

The day he left was a red-letter day in my life! I spent it in a total state of apprehension. Knowing Haiti, I was worried that he would have grave difficulty with his paperwork at the airport. His passport identified him as female, yet his appearance—with a beard, dreads, and masculine clothing—reflected his male identity. At that point, he had not changed all his paperwork to reflect his new status. He did have an official document from the doctor who had performed the mastectomy stating that he was transitioning. I was concerned about the reception he might face, knowing that attitudes toward gender identity can vary significantly in Haitian society. Thankfully, he was traveling with the son of a member of the diplomatic corps in Haiti, and they were whisked into a private room at the airport while they were being checked in, so a disaster was avoided. I don't think I took many breaths from the moment he left the house to when I heard from him that evening!

The following six months proved to be a significant learning curve for Sky as he navigated new cultural and personal challenges. There, he encountered the most rejection from everyone around him. It is known that Haitian society, in general, can be intolerant toward LGBTQ+ individuals. When he went, he was supposed to stay with some friends who had promised him a board until he got on his feet and found work. As they touched the Haitian soil, reality set in for them, and they said, "You're on your own," without a second thought. The betrayal Sky faced upon arrival in Haiti, abandoned by those he considered friends, was a harsh lesson in trust and resilience that deeply pained me as his mother. So there he was in a foreign land, barely speaking the local language. In a society that required name and connections, money, and diplomas, Sky stood out—and not in a good way. He had no diploma or specific trade (though he'd been trained in many different forms of manual labor). Instead, he had very little savings, dreadlocks, and an affinity to dress casually. Connections too, I imagine. Unfortunately, those shun him because of his status. Witnessing Sky's struggles in Haiti from afar, my heart ached with a mother's instinct to protect, yet I knew these trials were essential for his growth and self-discovery. I would have so wanted to shield him from this horrible reality of my country. I had foreseen this outcome. But he was learning.

Then came my brother-in-law, Fred, to save the day. How do you describe Fred? He was from Holland. He married my sister, and they moved to Haiti. He had an ironwork business. One day, one of his workers asked him, "So Fred, how come you act so differently from the other *blan*? Aren't you white?" His candid answer was, "No, I left this being white business a long time ago." That was Fred, a genuine human being, generous to a fault and authentic. So Sky stayed with him in a modest house he had built for himself. Fred, who'd picked up my son after his so-called friends left him stranded, generously shared his food, and provided employment through odd jobs, ensuring Sky's safe and stable stay in Haiti. Sky's limited interaction with our family and friends in Haiti underscored the painful reality of societal and familial rejection, a sobering reminder of the challenges he still faced. To this day, he insists it was an excellent opportunity for him. This unfortunate experience made him stronger and taught him to stand erect.

In a quest for personal growth, Sky embarked on a pilgrimage in 2018, walking 500 miles across Spain, from Saint Jean Pied de Port in France to Santiago de Compostela in Spain. It was the right moment in his life to do this; I see it. He met many pilgrims with whom he formed a profound connection—people of all ages, races, and nationalities. Sky is truly a "people person." Toward the end of the walk, he met with a group of young people with whom he connected, and they did the last week or so together. He introduced himself as Sky, and although he noticed a hint of curiosity in their expression about his background, he chose not to elaborate. Then, one day, he went on his Instagram to show them something, and they saw his profile picture, which is a double-sided picture of him: on one side, five-year-old Sole in her Girl Scout uniform; on the other, Sky wearing the same Girl Scout apron he had on before in the same pose as Sole. They all exclaimed, "Ah! Ha! That explains it. We sensed something unique about you!" They recognized then that he was transgender. He told them he wanted to see if they would realize this about him. They completed the pilgrimage together, forging lasting friendships; some remain in touch with Sky, sharing a bond formed on that transformative journey.

My interactions with Sky's friends on social media connected me to his world and provided me with deeper insights into his journey, furthering my understanding and acceptance. They contacted me personally to comment on his engaging personality. Sky is a remarkable person, a genuine and open man who can make you feel whole and true. Following the challenging times of his youth, Sky had taken firm control of his life's direction, sure of his identity, direction, and aspirations. Now that he had overcome such difficult days, he felt well in his skin. His newfound confidence played a pivotal role in breaking down barriers, gradually influencing those initially hesitant to accept him fully.

12.
Love Ought to Be Enough

Back at home, reminders of Sole still adorn our walls. I asked Sky a few times, "Would you want us to take these photos down so there is no confusion?" His response has been, "Of course not." Getting rid of them would be denying Sole's existence. A young niece saw a picture of Sole once and asked us, "This is a girl. How can it be Uncle Skiz?" We gently explained that Sky was born looking like a girl, but as he grew up, he understood that he was a boy inside, and so he became who he is now—Sky, Uncle Skiz. She seemed satisfied. Maybe later on, a more elaborate answer will be necessary. But for now, love is enough.

At this point, our family broke the silence, and we engaged in more open and honest conversations about Sky's journey and our feelings. Kahlil told me one day, "What you must realize, Mom, is that your daughter Sole is dead, and now Sky, a son, has replaced her."

Jim Sinclair, an autism activist, challenges the perception of autism as a tragedy in his article published in the Autism Network International newsletter, *Our Voice*, Volume 1, Number 3, 1993. He sees parents suffering tremendously, not because their child is autistic but because they dearly wish they had a non-autistic child. He explains that when they are praying for a cure to autism, they are essentially hoping that the autistic child will change into someone else, a stranger who fits their expectations. This is where we were with Sky. As my understanding deepened, I realized that embracing Sky didn't mean erasing Sole but instead accepting that their evolution was necessary for a fulfilling life. I needed to be proud of his strength and courage in pursuing his true self.

Embracing our transgender child, family member, or friend with this mindset can help us move beyond sadness to acceptance. When I thought of our family, I had no sadness because I didn't lose a child. This journey of acceptance reminds me of a poignant article in the *Los Angeles Times* in October 2012, "A Transgender Story: My Daughter, My Son." The author, Ann Whitford Paul, writes: "I want to love the man my daughter has become, but floundering in the torrent of her change and my resistance to it, I fear I'll never make it across my river of anger and sorrow." The mother metaphorically laments, "A transgender child brings a parent face to face with the death of their expectations. The daughter I had known and loved was gone; a stranger with facial hair and a deep voice had taken her place." In her book, *The Argonauts*, Maggie Nelson is outraged at the idea that one person's liberation is another's loss. Just like Mrs. Whitford, the realization of the courage and the strength her daughter had to have to accomplish what she did is what helped her accept her son. I didn't want to mourn my beautiful Sole. What I wanted to do was to continue seeing the strength of character Sky had demonstrated at a very young age.

Reflecting on Sky's early childhood, I recall an anecdote when Sole was just two years old. My sister from Haiti came to visit. We got home from the airport, and she, so happy to bond with her little niece, quickly got out of the car to open the vehicle's back door, eager to help Sole down the back seat. Without a word, this little person gave her a stern look that said, "Back off. My mom will help me." My sister stepped aside without needing more and let me get Sole down. After a few minutes, though, Sole was all over Laurence, showing her the house. She always knew what she wanted and would never let herself be swayed one way or another. I couldn't wish this girl dead to make room for a young man who, on his pilgrimage on the Camino de Santiago, stopped some guys who insisted that a young lady traveling with them have more beer than was safe for her. He did so calmly, with the same quiet, insistent stare that she gave her aunt at age two.

They stopped harassing the young lady, and the day after, the group crowned him "Knight of the Day"!

We were initially somewhat skeptical about the YES Institute's influence on Sky. Mostly, it was the idea that his quest to become a boy was accepted too readily, too quickly. Attending my first meeting with the YES Institute was a mix of skepticism and curiosity. Confronted with their frank discussions on gender identity, I felt a whirlwind of emotions and discomfort to a burgeoning sense of awareness. The goal was to engage with the community to educate us about homosexuality and transgender identity and to learn to accept all kinds of people. To not judge or condemn. It was at this meeting I first heard the powerful phrase, "Would you rather have a dead child or a live trans one?" The YES Institute's focus on suicide prevention resonated deeply with me, especially considering the dark moments Sky faced. It underscored the critical need for support and acceptance in their—and our—journey. They talked about the pink/blue color choices that are so stereotypic. They gave the example of the prices of pink and blue razors. The razors are precisely the same, but the pink ones will cost more, and women will still buy them. No, not my experience. Getting ready for our pilgrimage walk in Spain, it was suggested that we have a mace spray. At the Bass store, they had pink and black ones. The pinks were more expensive. I chose the black one. At one time, there was a big push to raise neutral children, and there

12. LOVE OUGHT TO BE ENOUGH

was an advertisement for a "My Buddy" doll for either girl or boy. My oldest son had it on his Santa list at Christmas. I had no qualms about getting it for him, despite my husband's disagreement (dissatisfaction?). No, I was not impressed by their philosophy.

A turning point came with the distressing episode of Sole's suicide attempt. The support they showed her, and the family was unparalleled. I saw a group of people who believed in their philosophy and stood by it. From the director herself, Martha Fugate, to many of the staff members, they all came to visit Sole in the hospital. That's when I started to appreciate their work. As I said before, this was part of the start of my acceptance of what "Sky" was going through. Every one of them who came to visit had a clear intention: to make Sky understand the value of his life. They emphasized his importance in making life authentic, reinforcing that suicide had no place in his journey. They insisted that we all had our place in this world. It dawned on me that this was exactly it, what I felt about my Sky. *Yes, I would rather have a trans child than have a dead daughter.* Realizing Sole is not "dead" but has evolved into Sky with a personality that is more in accordance with his inner being was a critical moment of acceptance for me.

Their point was *no suicide*—not because suicide is terrible, but because this life needed a Sky in it. This philosophy shifted our focus from preventing a tragic outcome to celebrating Sky's unique and necessary role in our lives and the world. It redefined our approach, emphasizing the importance of nurturing his presence and potential. Their concern was genuine. Martha's insistence on Sky's value and her plea against suicide resonated strongly with me. She insisted that Sky first made the solemn promise not ever to consider suicide again, and if he ever felt himself stumbling, he would contact her first.

The YES Institute's influence extends beyond individual lives to shaping community attitudes, which is evident in their engaging workshops and inclusive initiatives across various social sectors. When I came back from India and Sky came back from Orlando, he joined the YES staff. Participating in the YES Institute's communication courses was transformative. They opened my eyes to new ways of understanding and connecting with Sky, facilitating a deeper bond based on respect and true acceptance. This allowed me to truly understand the work they were doing. I recognized then that they were not pushing the wrong diagnosis on the people who came to them but just fully accepting the identity you felt you had. It was this lack of judging that impressed me the most. When I showed hesitation in their stand, they acknowledged it without arguing that their point was better than mine. Though they felt my reticence in accepting Sky as a transman, they appreciated my input in all our conversations. They invited me to talk to parents of other trans teens of Haitian origin. It was always a welcome idea. They understood that as I got involved with other families going through the same hard transition, it was helping me work it out and also helping me understand a little better what Sky was going through. Each conversation with other families navigating similar paths shed light on my feelings, gradually guiding me from confusion and resistance to a deeper understanding and acceptance of Sky's truth. In helping them see where their loved one was, I also sorted out where our family was. I realized that we, as a family, had to open the dialog and be there for him in a more concrete way. This is what the YES Institute has done for us—break the silence and make us realize that Sky faces a very hostile world. He needs us more than any other child needs us. A couple of years ago, Sky came to visit me in school, and a student at the Reef saw him. She had met Sky at YES, which shows the lasting impact of his journey on others. When she found out he was my son, she was in awe of me being so proud and open to having a transgender child. She was having some difficulties at home for being accepted as a transwoman. She often came to visit me in my classroom, and we spoke. I encouraged her to be patient with her family. It is a hard concept to understand, but their love for her would eventually surface. By graduation, she triumphantly told me things were much better in the house. She was going to graduation in a gorgeous green dress! Deja vu? I was reminded of the wedding Sky had wanted to attend in a suit that had created such a commotion with the family! The YES Institute is involved in many aspects of the community; this is another layer of their work that I admire. Not only do they offer classes at the Institute directly, but they also go out in the community, schools, nursing homes, hospitals, and businesses to encourage people to accept each other and help us all understand what we are all about. They gave an interesting presentation at the University of Miami with a super cool ending. My young niece was taking a class at the university on women's studies, and the professor told them she had invited a transman to come and give a talk to the class. Raphaelle was very excited about the meeting since her cousin was transitioning, and she could ask the guest all the questions she'd never dared to ask her cousin. So, on the day of the visit, she had all her questions ready. And one after the other, she bombarded the guest with questions! Her professor and the other students were a little puzzled at her great interest in the subject. Until it dawned on them that she knew a transman. And the best part was when their guest realized the cousin was none other than his roommate, Sky!

13.
My Sole, My Sky

Here we are, my Sole, my Sky. On this journey we started so many years ago, I've pondered the questions that have shaped our family. How has your transition changed us? What have we learned? Where are we as a family in your transition? Will these questions ever be wholly answered?

Much of this has been thoughtfully considered in my mind—and I dedicate this book to you, to the family, to our friends, to all those embracing the reality of having a trans person in their lives, to those, like my mother's friend, who struggle with understanding this reality, who see it as a "coffin in their living room."

Sole, I have reflected deeply on the reality of losing you. I still wonder if personal identity is more than societal stereotypes, especially in your experience. What does it mean for you, my Sole, my sunshine, to be who you truly are? How do I understand the idea of death foretold by your name?

Sky, how did you come to understand your true self? Know that while I miss the presence of my daughter, Sole, and hold dear the memories of that past self, I embrace and fully accept you, my son, my Sky, recognizing that you two are intertwined. You both embody the same spirit that brightened our lives from the moment you were born on April 6, 1991, regardless of gender identity. I love the multifaceted person you are.

My Sole, my Sky, one revelation that has struck me is that you have navigated much of this journey with great personal courage. Gradually, I've come to appreciate your immense strength and resilience. Despite adversity or lack of understanding from others, you have remained true to yourself and emerged with dignity and grace. Sky, I look at this young person you are, and I feel absolutely no regrets. Over time, I've grown proud of your integrity and the resolve you've shown to always stay strong in the face of hardship, which you have experienced and will again, to be sure.

Challenges from those who do not yet understand will arise, as well as friends not ready to acknowledge the changes you have undergone. In the documentary *Prodigal Sons*, the author, Kimberly Reed, a transwoman, shares her experience of returning to her hometown and finding unexpected acceptance. I wish you had experienced that with the youth group you belonged to, instead of the lack of recognition you were given when the other group members were being recognized later on in life. I am aware that there have been, and there will be again, moments of pain and loneliness. I cannot protect you from all life's hardships, but I hope you know I will always be here for you, ready to offer support, love, and guidance.

Sky, the dream I had for Sole, I still have for you—a wish for companionship and support through life's moments, someone who will celebrate the triumphs alongside you. My concern for you stems from a place of deep love. While it may be difficult, finding a partner who understands and supports you would be a source of immense joy and comfort. Yet, remember that fulfillment and happiness also come from love and connections with family and friends.

You've had two meaningful relationships in your life. I remember Julia fondly. You were very young at the time. Her mother was a very warm woman and very supportive of her daughter. I remember her puzzlement when you declared yourself a transman and not a lesbian. She asked me one day: "What does that make Julia then?! Is she still a lesbian?" We had a good laugh about it—two mothers trying to understand the complicated lives of their children. I am grateful that you both remain on good terms. Then, there was Ebonie. I liked her immediately. Not only was she an intelligent young woman, but she also seemed to care for you. I immediately sensed the positive energy between you two. You both seemed to look out for each other in a kind way. I liked that. I secretly hoped that your bond would solidify into something everlasting. When it didn't, I felt a pang of sadness. But more than anything, I worry about your future. However, I remain hopeful that the right person will come into your life and bring you the happiness and companionship you deserve.

Above all else, Sky, please know that I am proud of who you are and grateful to have you as my child. Reflecting on your journey, I've found it awe-inspiring, and I will continue to be by your side, supporting and loving you always with deep understanding and compassion. You empowered yourself to transition, Sole, Sky—despite the roadblocks, despite the silence. I deeply admire the clarity and conviction you've shown. The fact that we did not participate fully in your journey gave you time to assert yourself and be sure of your path. The fundraiser for the mastectomy gave you complete ownership of this transition. Sole or Sky, my love for you remains unchanged. I love Sole. I love Sky. Sole will always be my daughter. Sky will always be my son.

Despite my struggle, I see you as a person beyond the simple binary of male and female. No matter what, my love for you is unwavering and absolute.

14.
Bridging Perspectives

I want to share a very personal letter I wrote to my friends and family, along with their responses, to give you a fuller picture of the journey my family and I have been on with my transgender child, Sky. This letter wasn't just an update; it was an invitation for those closest to us to reflect on their own experiences, feelings, and thoughts about Sky's transition and the broader questions it raised about identity and acceptance.

I asked them several questions, aiming to understand their initial reactions, how those feelings may have evolved over time, their struggles with changing pronouns, and their general views on LGBTQ+ issues. This wasn't an easy letter to write. It laid bare not only Sky's vulnerabilities but also my own, as I navigated my role as a mother through uncharted territories.

The responses I received were varied, illuminating the wide spectrum of human emotions and reactions. Some were supportive from the start, while others needed time to adjust their understanding and acceptance. This diversity of responses underscored for me the complexity of the human experience—how we deal with change, confront our biases, and ultimately, how we grow in love and understanding.

By sharing these interactions in the book, I aim not just to tell my story or Sky's story but to highlight the shared human experience behind it. It's about more than just the challenges we faced; it's about the conversations, the moments of doubt, the misunderstandings, and the breakthroughs.

Including these voices in my narrative serves a dual purpose. It paints a fuller picture of the societal landscape regarding transgender issues and underscores the individual and collective journey toward understanding and acceptance. It's a reminder that while our experiences may differ, at the core, we're all navigating the complexities of life and identity, trying to understand each other better and support the ones we love.

This is not just a recount of events; it's an invitation to you, the reader, to engage with these stories, reflect on your perceptions, and perhaps see the world through a slightly different lens. Through this honest and open exchange,

14. BRIDGING PERSPECTIVES

I hope to contribute to the broader conversation about gender, identity, and acceptance, encouraging empathy and understanding in a world that desperately needs more of both.

Letter from Isabelle

Hello to all,

Some of you might be aware already that I am writing a reflection on being the mother of a transgender child. The idea had come to me quite a few years ago after reading an article a mother had written about the despair she felt when her teenage daughter announced she wanted to transition into a boy. Speaking to my cousin about it, she casually said, "You like to write. Why don't you write a book about your experience?" The idea was planted then. But life happens! You all know my long hours when I was teaching! Then retirement came, and then I had oodles of time... so back on the idea!

I am diligently working on the project now.

Today, I realized that all of you are part of this journey that Sky is going through, and I thought I'd like to include your thoughts in my book. As family and friends, how are we coping and understanding this? So, totally voluntarily, if you would let me know in a few words, a paragraph, or 1,000 words 😊, what your thoughts are on his transformation.

    In the beginning, what was your reaction?
    As time went by, have you changed your mind?
    Do you still see Sole sometimes?
    Any regrets at the loss of her?
    Have your feelings for "her" changed for "him"?
    Is it difficult to change the pronoun?
    Do you still make the mistake?
    How do you feel if you slip and say "Sole" or "she"?
    Now, not regarding Sky himself, what is your general feeling about LGBTQ+ 🏳️‍🌈?

Three things:

Of course you do NOT have to answer. Truly.

If you would rather have a conversation about it with me, give me a call, come over (ha! ALL THE WAY TO SoBe?!! 🤷 😅 😊) or ask me to come to you.

If you would rather not include your name, it is perfectly ok 👍, absolutely.

I think it will be a very valuable part of the book, so please, if you're ok to let me know your thoughts, I will be very excited and grateful.

As you can imagine, this has been a very difficult and harsh journey for us. Do you remember Tante Danne, Evna's mother? Way at the beginning, one of my nephews was getting married in New York, and as we were all getting ready to go, Sky announced he was going dressed as a man, suit and tie! I panicked! I was so distraught! Well, Tante Danne, an old woman, devout Catholic, extremely religious, put some perspective for me in a way I will never forget! She simply said, "Bello, as much as you think you love your child, know that God loves him more." And that's when slowly a shift started happening in me.

Did you have such a moment too?

For those of you with young children, an interesting incident occurred last weekend at the house. Colbert and Cecile were here with their daughters. Olivia (9) saw a picture of young Sole. She was flabbergasted! "But that's a girl!" she exclaimed. 😳😨 I left it for them to talk to her about it. How will you tell your young child that "Uncle Skiz" was actually "Aunt Sole" once, if they ask?

I am putting a date on this, not to put pressure on you, but to let you know it's okay if you don't want to write. Not to let the thought linger too long. You either want to say your piece simply or you don't. Answer my questions simply or say your own thoughts. No judgment whatsoever. Again, a sentence or two or 1,000 😄☺—by next week?

I love you all,
Isabelle
P.S. Thank you for being part of the journey!

The Response

From Hilde:

Isabelle,

What a wonderful project you've embarked on. I can't wait to see it published—I'm certain it will be! Reflecting back, I vaguely remember our phone conversation where you mentioned a girlfriend and Sky's name change while he was still in high school. My initial, misguided reaction was to blame his friends, thinking they were influencing him, which embarrasses me now. The change to a unisex name like Sky didn't strike me as significant then, largely because I was uninformed about transgender issues. My knowledge was limited to gays and lesbians, without understanding the profound struggle of feeling misaligned with one's physical gender. Looking back, I see our generation's lack of education and the biases we held.

I regret not being there for you and Pantal during those challenging times. However, the moment you shared that family photo, acknowledging you have four sons, it touched me deeply. It was a beautiful declaration of acceptance and love. Strangely enough, I have yet to properly meet Sky. The last time we visited Miami, he was away. We must remedy this soon.

With affection,

Hilde

14. BRIDGING PERSPECTIVES

From Klawdia:

Isabelle,

I've often put myself in your shoes, wondering, "What would I do?" Accepting Sky was not difficult for me, but it did spark my curiosity. He was quite open about his transition, especially significant changes like top surgery. No question was too silly for him to answer. Over the years, my feelings have evolved; while I wasn't particularly close to Sole, Sky has become very dear to me. His journey makes me wonder about the challenges he faces, silently or otherwise. His story, and now your book, highlight the complexity of such experiences. It's not just a story of change but one of profound personal growth and societal impact.

From Fédora:

Isabelle,

The world is gradually becoming more accepting of differences, and that's heartening. Faith in God and allowing Sky to pursue his happiness are what matter. Your unconditional love is the constant he needs. Seeing pictures of you all always warms my heart. Best wishes to both Kahlil and Sky.

From Diana:

> Dear Bouboule,
> Your willingness to share your journey and invite us into it is moving. I feel honored to be considered a part of this narrative. Blessings to you and your family for the courage and love you've shown.

From Nini:

> Isabelle,
> This has been a touching read. Sky's transition was hard for everyone, not just him. In a world so full of negativity, why add more toward someone we love? I'm thankful for the progress made and that Sky has found his place. Love is powerful, and I believe it will lead us to understanding.

From Chris:

> Hi Aunt Isabelle,
> Sky living his truth has never been an issue for me. Supporting Kevin was just as natural as supporting Sky. People deserve to live their lives freely. Sky has my unwavering support.

14. BRIDGING PERSPECTIVES

From Liline:

Bello, I have always understood that some individuals are born unique, and your child is a shining example of this. This awareness has cultivated my tolerance. Breaking through the barriers of prejudice is a challenging and enduring task. We cannot fully comprehend what those who are different from us experience, as we do not inhabit their bodies. Such differences are determined by forces beyond our control. Judgment is not our place. Although we have never explicitly discussed this, I have always admired your courage, strength, and maternal love in supporting your child through their journey. The book you are writing is a commendable effort that will undoubtedly assist other mothers and society at large. A testament to the need for greater tolerance in our world. Our family has always supported you, albeit silently. Lastly, seeing Sky at Elfried's funeral was a delight; our brief interaction was warmly received. I eagerly await your book.

Love,
Liline

From Melina:

Reflecting on when I learned Sky identified as male, my initial thought was sympathy for Tante Bouboule, who, after three boys, finally had a daughter who didn't identify with being a girl. I fondly recalled our shopping trips and salon visits in Miami, saddened by the thought she couldn't share these moments with her daughter. However, Sole's preference for traditionally male interests and attire and her attraction to girls never troubled me.

Embracing Sky's identity was seamless for me, although adjusting to his new name took some effort. Sky's transition prompted me to contemplate my understanding and acceptance of transgender individuals, realizing my primary concern was for Sky's happiness and comfort.

Several questions arose, challenging my acceptance. First, I believe that God's creation is infallible. If so, how can someone feel misplaced in their body? I also struggled to understand societal resistance to accepting transgender individuals. Finally, I wondered about the intrinsic value of aligning one's gender identity with their inner sense of self.

Despite these questions, my support for Sky never wavered. Adapting to his physical changes, particularly noticing feminine features beneath his beard, was initially challenging. Over time, however, Sky's identity solidified for me, overshadowing any remnants of Sole.

Observing Kahlil's adjustment to losing his sister was difficult, highlighting the complex dynamics of change within familial relationships. My bond with Sky has only strengthened, devoid of any longing for Sole. My hope is for a world that embraces Sky, allowing him to live authentically.

While full comprehension may elude me, my unwavering support for Sky remains, rooted in love.

From Raphaëlle:

Initially, Sky's transition was a mix of confusion and surprise for me, given the lack of open discussions about such topics in our culture. Over time, witnessing Isabelle's public acceptance and developing a closer relationship with Sky as an adult reinforced the importance of personal connections over societal norms.

The memory of Sole is distant, overshadowed by my stronger, adult connection with Sky. The occasional slip in pronouns is a challenge, highlighting the ongoing need for explanation and acceptance in social contexts.

My views on the LGBTQ+ community, informed by my academic background in Women and Gender Studies, reflect a broad acceptance and curiosity about evolving social norms. Despite this, the prospect of navigating non-traditional situations with my future children underscores the complexity of acceptance on a personal level.

From Carole :

Choosing to write is a brilliant decision. It serves as both a method to structure your thoughts and an opportunity to reflect on your emotions. Additionally, writing can act as a form of catharsis or therapeutic release. There are numerous benefits to writing a book, not only for personal growth but also for its potential to help others, regardless of whether they share similar experiences. Life presents us with unexpected challenges that we must learn to accept. The reasons behind these challenges are known only to God. My personal views on the LGBTQ+ movement aside, I have never thought to link Sky with it. To me, Sky has always been someone who bravely acknowledges and lives his truth, regardless of the potential repercussions for himself, our family, and our friends. I fondly recall Sole as an infant, offering my little finger for comfort in the absence of a milk bottle. I also cherish the memory of Sky supporting Gisele and me at our brother Patrick's funeral, where his presence was a source of strength. May God grant you the courage to endure, heal your wounds, and unveil the purpose of this challenging chapter in your life. I look forward to your book with great anticipation.

Warmest regards,
Carole

14. BRIDGING PERSPECTIVES

Pétunia C.:

Hi Bello,

Writing down your experiences can be a healing process, and I'm pleased you're embarking on this journey. My only memory of Sole was during a brief visit to Miami, where I met my little cousin. It wasn't until I saw Sky on Facebook that I understood the change. Sole is a distant memory, and I fully embrace and recognize Sky as he is now. The video you shared about a family's experience with a transgender child brought home the reality of your situation. I hold no judgment, only acceptance. We're all born with our unique traits; some conform to societal expectations, while others navigate their distinct paths. Such journeys are challenging due to societal attitudes and beliefs. I wish you and Sky all the best.

Movements like the LGBTQ+ are crucial for fostering change, despite occasionally overstepping boundaries. Ultimately, they contribute to societal progress.

From Yotty & GM Celestin:

I'll never forget my first encounter with Sky—an incredible individual. Sky visited my workplace, The Lotus House, to give a presentation. His eloquence, confidence, and openness about his life's struggles made a lasting impression.

Sky's transparency was empowering. After his presentation, I felt compelled to speak with him. During our conversation, Sky shared the difficulties his family faced in accepting his identity, emphasizing that his transition was not a choice but a reflection of his true self. Discovering Sky's parents, Isabelle and Pantal, whom I knew from Spring Valley, was a surprising connection that brought joy to our interaction. Sky's proud and joyful reaction to our shared history highlighted his genuine spirit. My admiration for Sky's courage, dignity, persistence, and loving heart has only grown. Sky, you are truly remarkable, a beautiful creation of God.

I am honored to know you and have you in my life. You are amazing!

With love and admiration,
Yotty & GM Celestin

Wider Shifts Ahead

I was struck by the depth of honesty, vulnerability, and love reflected in the responses to my letter from friends and family. Their insights not only share the journey of understanding and accepting Sky's transition but also reflect wider shifts in societal attitudes toward transgender individuals and the LGBTQ+ community.

14. BRIDGING PERSPECTIVES

The varied reactions—from initial surprise to deep acceptance—reveal the changing nature of human relationships and social norms. This dialogue opens a door to the complexities of navigating gender identity within family and community contexts, showing that acceptance and understanding evolve over time, nurtured by patience, learning, and open-hearted discussions.

By sharing these personal stories, we've initiated a conversation that underscores the importance of connection and support in facing the challenges of gender identity. The responses from my loved ones demonstrate society's capacity for change and compassion, highlighting the journey from misunderstanding to advocacy.

Sole's Mom celebrates the power of sharing our true selves and the impact it can have on fostering a more inclusive and supportive world. It's a call to recognize the strength of openness and the profound effect of empathetic listening and dialogue.

I am deeply thankful to my friends, family, and you, the reader, for joining us on this path. Your engagement, curiosity, and willingness to confront challenging discussions contribute immeasurably to our collective journey toward a more accepting society.

I hope the experiences and reflections shared here inspire ongoing conversations about identity and acceptance. Let's move forward with the lessons of love and support that have emerged from these pages, committed to understanding and celebrating each individual for who they truly are.

Thank you for being a part of this meaningful exploration. Your readiness to engage and learn is a powerful force for positive change. Let us continue to carry the spirit of these conversations into our lives, always remembering the value of recognizing and honoring each other's true selves.

With gratitude and optimism,

Isabelle

About the Author

Isabelle Camille is an accomplished educator with over thirty-four years of experience at Miami-Dade County Public Schools and as an adjunct professor at Miami Dade College. With a bachelor of science in chemistry from the University of Florida and a master of education in science teacher education from Florida International University, her commitment to education and her impactful work have earned her recognition, including being an honored listee in Marquis Who's Who. Fluent in French and Haitian Creole, Isabelle is also passionate about community outreach, curriculum development, and educational technology. Her personal journey with her transgender child has transformed her into a passionate advocate for LGBTQ+ rights, actively participating in support groups and working closely with organizations like the YES Institute to promote awareness and empathy for transgender individuals and their families. Isabelle's dedication to fostering inclusive and understanding environments both in her professional and personal life underscores her commitment to making a positive impact in the world.

Made in the USA
Columbia, SC
27 March 2025